Java

Chris Wright

TEACH YOURSELF BOOKS

For UK orders: please contact Bookpoint Ltd, 39 Milton Park, Abingdon, Oxon OX14 4TD. Telephone: (44) 01235 400414, Fax: (44) 01235 400454. Lines are open from 9.00 – 6.00, Monday to Saturday, with a 24 hour message answering service. Email address: orders@bookpoint.co.uk

For U.S.A. & Canada orders: please contact NTC/Contemporary Publishing, 4255 West Touhy Avenue, Lincolnwood, Illinois 60646 – 1975 U.S.A. Telephone: (847) 679 5500, Fax: (847) 679 2494.

Long renowned as the authoritative source for self-guided learning – with more than 30 million copies sold worldwide – the *Teach Yourself* series includes over 200 titles in the fields of languages, crafts, hobbies, sports, and other leisure activities.

British Library Cataloguing in Publication Data
A catalogue record for this title is available from The British Library

Library of Congress Catalog Card Number: 98-65905

First published in UK 1998 by Hodder Headline Plc, 338 Euston Road, London NW1 3BH

First published in US 1998 by NTC/Contemporary Publishing, 4255 West Touhy Avenue, Lincolnwood (Chicago), Illinois 60646 – 1975 U.S.A.

The 'Teach Yourself' name and logo are registered trade marks of Hodder & Stoughton Ltd.

Copyright © 1998 Chris Wright

In UK: All rights reserved. No part of this publication may be reproduced or transmitted in any form or by any means, electronic or mechanical, including photocopy, recording, or any information storage and retrieval system, without permission in writing from the publisher or under licence from the Copyright Licensing Agency Limited. Further details of such licences (for reprographic reproduction) may be obtained from the Copyright Licensing Agency Limited, of 90 Tottenham Court Road, London W1P 9HE.

In US: All rights reserved. No part of this book may be reproduced, stored in a retrieval system, or transmitted in any form, or by any means, electronic, mechanical, photocopying, or otherwise, without prior permission of NTC/Contemporary Publishing Company.

Typeset by MacDesign, Southampton.
Printed in Great Britain for Hodder & Stoughton Educational, a division of Hodder Headline Plc, 338 Euston Road, London NW1 3BH by Cox & Wyman Ltd, Reading, Berkshire.

Impression number	10	9	8	7	6	5	4	3	2	
Year		2004	2003	2002	2001	2000	1999	1998		

CONTENTS

ACKNOWLEDGEMENTS

Of the many products referred to in this book, those that are registered trademarks are acknowledged as being the property of their owners.

Sun Microsystems, Unix, SunSoft, Java, JavaScript, Netscape, Microsoft, MSDOS, Windows, Windows 95, Paintshop Pro, Graphics Workshop

Thanks are also due to Benny Faria at Sun, the staff and students of the School of Informatics and Multimedia Technology at the University of North London, Matt Mower and Mike O'Reilly at ISS, and Brenda McWalters for their support throughout the course of this project.

DISCLAIMER

Feel free to use any of the code you find in this book. This is a book to be treated as you would a recipe book – some of the dishes are complex, others are not. Be aware that if you do use code from this book, all of the programs have been written to show how a part of the language works. For this reason, error checking, which is a vital part of industrial strength programming, has been kept to a minimum. Bear in mind that you must provide for user mistakes as well as computer problems. For example the Calculator program (Chapter 3) would in the real world test for the user inputting invalid data, the Web browser (Chapter 9) would test for the user growing impatient and sending a second request before the first has been dealt with. This type of eventuality can cause serious problems, so ignore at your peril!

1

GETTING STARTED

1.1 Aims of this chapter

This book is aimed at people with some knowledge of computing at an introductory level, who have experience of surfing the web, have come across Java and who wish to take things a stage further. You will discover what Java is, how it relates to JavaScript, where it comes from, how to obtain it and install it and what hardware and additional software you need to run it.

1.2 What is Java?

Java is a large language, and it is not my intention with this book to cover all of it. Rather I want to provide the basic building blocks and to introduce a method of working which allows the user to create working applets and applications.

Java is a portable, interpreted, object oriented programming language. It is *portable* in that the same program will run on any platform running the Java Virtual Machine (JVM) – unlike C++ for example which has to be recompiled for every platform. The JVM is the software that interprets our programs for the operating system. This gives the language a considerable advantage because code need only be written once – saving development time, and because we can send a Java program to any computer without worrying about whether it will work or not. On the Internet, this gives Java a unique advantage.

It is *interpreted*, in that when a Java program is compiled, it is compiled to bytecode, rather than machine code. It is this characteristic that gives it portability, but it is achieved at the cost of speed. You can view bytecode as a 'half way house' between the original program and the machine instructions that actually run the computer. It is the responsibility of the JVM to interpret the bytecode for the specific platform.

It is *object oriented*. The development of programming languages can be seen as a journey away from the machine – Assembler language – towards the Human way of doing things. Object Orientation is an attempt to mimic the way that humans see the world. The theory is that if we can do this successfully, then designing a computer program should become an intuitive as well as an intellectual exercise. Objects can be viewed as components and if we look at the construction industry – one of the oldest human activities, we see that the component idea has been around for a long time. If we are building a house, and need a water supply, we send for the plumber. In programming terms the plumber would be an object, knowing the detail about water in houses. We, as the architect don't need to know the details, only the plumber's phone number. We will be looking more closely at object orientation in Chapter 3.

Java is not to be confused with JavaScript. JavaScript is an interpreted scripting language which is object based and uses similar programming techniques. JavaScript is used exclusively as a Web based tool to enhance the interaction of Web pages viewed in a browser such as Netscape or Internet Explorer. Although there are similarities between the two, Java is a much more powerful tool for the Web developer.

—1.3 The future – Java Beans, JDBC—

Trends noticeable in the present include the widespread use of *intranets* within corporate computing. The use of intranets invites widespread dissemination of information through the use of databases. All information retrievable from a company's computer will be current. There will be no more generations of paper memos to juggle. Java provides methods to seamlessly integrate relational databases into the web browser, so the browser becomes the front end for a database.

JDBC stands for Java Database Connectivity. Current trends imply that much Web content will be supplied by large databases storing and manipulating data as it becomes available. This normally requires some sort of 'middleware' to govern the process of a web browser 'talking to' a database. Java 1.1 provides a new package, **java.sql** which allows the programmer to directly interrogate a relational database in the language it understands – SQL. The JDBC provides a set of APIs (Application Programming Interfaces) that make this process a simple one of transferring data between databases and Java objects.

There is also a demand for less programmer-intensive languages. The success of Visual programming and the widespread use of 4GLs has made rapid application development a reality. Java is not a visual programming environment, although such IDEs (Integrated Development Environments) are available. What Java offers is an advanced (and still evolving) set of packages containing ready-made objects for programmers to use. The Java AWT (Abstract Windows Toolkit), for example, provides widgets in the form of scroll bars, menus, dialogue boxes, etc. which can be easily integrated into programs and which are guaranteed to run on any platform supporting the Java Virtual Machine. Sun have recently brought Java closer to the 4GL way of working with the introduction in JDK1.1 of JavaBeans.

JavaBeans is a framework for defining reusable, modular software components. The specification says that a Java Bean is a reusable software component that can be manipulated visually in a builder tool. Java beans can be customised, their properties altered and reused in a specific program. The builder tool is called a Bean Box. At the lowest level, reuse is already provided for in the shape of AWT components such as scroll bars, text fields, etc. JavaBeans will enable reuse at a much higher level. We will be able to package high level components as Beans and therefore reduce our development costs. Java Beans is likely to combine the power of 4GL rapid application development tools with the flexibility of an object oriented programming language in a way that Microsoft have only hinted at with Visual Basic and ActiveX.

1.4 Where can I get Java?

If your operating system is Windows NT or 95, Macintosh or Solaris, you can download Java free from Sun at:

http://www.javasoft.com/

If your operating system is Linux, you will require a port of the JDK designed for that operating system. Information on current ports can be found at the Blackdown Organisation's Web site:

http://www.blackdown.org/

The current version of Java is found in the Java Developers' Kit (JDK) version 1.1.3. This release contains some substantial improvements over release 1.0, most notably in the areas of Event Handling (Chapter 8) and Communications (Chapter 9). Where improvements are intended to replace version 1.0 methods, the older methods are said to be *deprecated* (disapproved of), but are still supported at the time of writing. In other words, both standards will work if your JDK is version 1.1 upwards, but version 1.0 will only support the deprecated versions.

If we were writing applications only, this confusion would be simply dealt with by using methods from JDK1.1 only. Applets however, depend on the browser to interpret the code and it is here that the state of the art lags behind the language implementation. If our goal is that everyone can view our applets then it is advised to use methods from version 1.0 in applet programming, until we are confident that every desktop computer has a 1.1 compatible browser.

This book is therefore based around version 1.0, with sections on 1.1 where Event handling and Communications are concerned.

You will require the README file which comes in the JDK bundle. This contains explicit instructions on installation. It is also viewable on the Javasoft web site at:

http://www.javasoft.com/products/jdk/1.1/docs/index.html

You may also decide to download the Java Beans Development Kit (BDK). This is an extension to the language enabling developers to define and use their own custom components. Java Beans are a more advanced subject than this book will cover.

——1.5 What equipment do I need?——

You need to have a PC running Windows NT or Windows 95, equipped with 16 Mb memory and a 486 processor or better. You will require 50 Mb of free disk space. You may also run the JDK on a Power Mac or Apple Macintosh using System 7.5.3 revision 2 or above. All these platforms, in addition to Unix are supported by Sunsoft. If you are running Linux on a x486 PC you should refer to back Section 1.3 for information.

—1.6 How do I learn to program Java?—

Java is not a difficult language to learn, but it is a difficult language to master. The reality is that learning to program is more unforgiving than learning a language, but shares with linguistics the ability to build abstractions out of small structures governed by rigid syntactical rules. The key to learning to program is confidence and for that reason, this book focuses on programs that you might encounter in the real world, rather than on programs which are artificially contrived to illustrate a point about programming technique. I have used this type of program only where there is a danger that a vital point may be lost if embedded in a larger program. Chapter 2, for example, where the ground rules are established, contains little in the way of real world examples.

The traditional method of learning to program was that the basic skills were taught first, then the programmer would work checking and correcting other people's code for a period, until their employer decided they could be trusted to write code themselves. The benefit of this was that the programmer would see how experienced programmers dealt with the language and, in particular, how they used the language to solve abstract problems. For this reason, many of the chapters begin with fairly advanced examples. Do not worry if you don't understand the example straight away. The important thing is that you try to trace the logic of the program as you work through the chapter. All should be clear in the end.

This book, used in isolation, will not teach you to be a programmer. It will teach you several things about Java, but you need to supplement the book with practice – do attempt the exercises, as they are designed to allow you to build upon the 'story so far', and often draw on techniques demonstrated in earlier chapters.

To get the best out of the language, the reader should join at least one newsgroup, and bookmark several of the reference sites indicated in Appendix 2. Java can be a complex language and you will save much time by referring to the Java API (see Exercise 1.6), which lists all of the packages supplied with Java and more importantly, lists the methods available to each class, indicating argument types and return types (see page 12).

1.7 Summary

Java is a programming language, not an application. Like all programming languages it possesses its own rules governing syntax and grammar, but unlike many it provides extensive libraries of predefined classes allowing the programmer the best of the 'plug in and play' approach typified by 4GLs, combined with the flexibility and power of languages such as C++.

Java is distributed free by Sun Microsystems. It was designed originally as a language to use to enable electronic components to communicate. The Internet provided the perfect opportunity for Java as a language and Sun as a company to put up a viable alternative to Microsoft's dominance of the PC world.

There is more information published about Java than an other aspect of computing except the World Wide Web itself. This is a measure of how enthusiastically people have responded to the existence of a truly multi-platform programming language.

In order to learn to program, you have to program – this cannot be understated. It is only by use that you will become fluent in Java. Many of the exercises in the book are designed for you to develop and customise for your own use.

1.8 Exercises

1. Download Java from the Sun web site at:
   http://www.javasoft.com/
2. Print out the ReadMe files and read them!
3. Install Java on your computer.
4. Join the news groups **comp.lang.java.programmer** and **comp.lang.java.gui**
5. Bookmark the Gamelan web site at:
   http://www.gamelan.com/
6. Bookmark the Java API Guide. This is generally supplied by Sun with the distribution and, if you installed the JDK in C:\, it can be found in **C:\jdk1.1.2\docs\api**. Start at **packages.html**.

   If you have not downloaded the documentation, it can be found at Sun's Web site:

   http://java.sun.com/products/jdk/1.1/docs/api/packages.html

2

PROGRAMMING BASICS

2.1 Aims of this chapter

The primary aim of this chapter is to create and compile simple Java programs.

In order to succeed in this we need to look at the language syntax and to understand the meaning and functions of data types, key words (see appendix 1), the use of variables, operators and the concept and practice of program control. We will introduce each new concept by looking at the way that it works inside a program. You can compile the programs and then you will see the effect of altering certain statements within the program. The examples will illustrate the use of various language elements and we can use the examples as a basis for building larger programs.

There are exercises at the end of the chapter. Try to complete these – you may have to search through the book in order to find solutions to some of the problems. Don't worry if you have trouble with some questions. You can always come back to them later.

Answers to the programming exercises can be found on my web site at

http://www.unl.ac.uk/~cwright/tyj/

———— 2.2 A first Java program ————

This section assumes that you are working with Windows 95. The commands which are represented in italics are the same for all versions of the JDK, whether your platform is Unix, Windows 95 or Apple.

For best results, use multiple windows, one to edit in, one to compile and one to run the programs. This practice will save you time, because you can use the right-hand arrow key on the keyboard to repeat the previous command.

Open a DOS window and type:

```
edit MyFirst.java
```

Now enter the code below, exactly as it is written here.

```
/* This is my first program. It is designed to
demonstrate a simple program structure
Author: Chris Wright 11.02.97 */

import java.io.*;

class MyFirst
{
    public static void main(String[ ] args)
    {
        System.out.println ("Hello Birds, Hello Sky!!");
    }
}
```

Save the file and compile the program in a second DOS window. Change directories until you are in the same directory as your program file, then enter at the command prompt the line:

```
javac MyFirst.java
```

If you have entered the file correctly, you should receive no error message. If you have made a mistake, you will get a message in the format:

```
MyFile.java:7: missing {
```

This would tell you that you have missed out a bracket on line 7. If this is the case, alter your source file, save it and recompile the program.

If your compilation is successful, run the program (from a third window) by entering the line:

java MyFirst

You should see a line of text printed to the screen, saying:

Hello Birds, Hello Sky!!

The line:

System.out.println ("Hello Birds, Hello Sky!!");

is the one which determines the actual output. If you alter the text between the inverted commas, you will get a different message when you recompile and run the program.

Let's first examine the syntax. To make this clear, we will build the program up from the statement that prints to the screen.

System.out.println ("Hello Birds, Hello Sky!!");

The line is terminated by a semi-colon. This tells the computer that it is a complete instruction.

The brackets contain that which is to be printed – in effect we are passing the contents of the brackets to the method **println**. The quote marks indicate the beginning and end of a **String** which will be reproduced exactly on the screen, without the quote marks. Note that a space is treated as a character in the representation of Strings.

The dots separating the words **System**, **out** and **println** indicate a relationship between the three words. Here we are using the **System** object with its variable **out** which is an object of type **PrintStream**. This means we can use the **PrintStream** method **println()**. The relationship and uses of classes and methods will be explained in detail in Chapter 3.

```
public static void main(String[] args)
{
    System.out.println ("Hello Birds, Hello Sky!!");
}
```

The curly brackets enclose a block of statements that belong to the method **main**. In this case there is only one statement, but we could have several, each one terminated by a semi-colon.

The ordinary brackets containing the words **String[] args** have exactly the same function as the brackets containing the **Hello Birds..** message. We are passing the contents of these brackets to the method. In this case though, we are passing a variable (which may contain a value) instead of an actual value. The variable in this usage is a list of arguments which we have called **args**. The term *argument* or *parameter* is used to describe information passed to a method or class in this way. The square brackets are used to indicate that this particular argument is a list (see **Array** page 26 and **String** page 15). This usage is unique in Java in that it is always used with the method main, regardless of whether we want to pass an argument to the method or not.

The words public static and void are also mandatory with the main method. Their effect in turn is to make the contents of main accessible to the whole programme (public), to ensure that the method exists in memory for the entire duration of the program (static) and to indicate that the method will not be returning any data for further processing (void) .

```
class MyFirst
{
    public static void main(String[] args)
    {
        System.out.println ("Hello Birds, Hello Sky!!");
    } // end of method

} // end of class
```

The name *myFirst* is provided by the programmer. Ideally names provided for methods, classes and variables should be descriptive, methods and classes are often described with composite names, the first letter of the second part being capitalised to enhance readability. It is also permissable to use capitals and the underscore character to link two words but as this practice is used by the creators of Java to indicate Events (eg **WINDOW_DESTROY** which refers to the event caused by someone closing a window) it is usually avoided by programmers. The curly bracket under the class MyFirst line indicates the beginning of the method definitions of a class (see Chapter 3). This is exactly the same usage as with the inner set of curly brackets. The definitions are terminated by the last curly bracket.

```
import java.io.*;
class MyFirst
{
   public static void main(String[] args)
   {
      System.out.println ("Hello Birds, Hello Sky!!");
   } // end of method

} // end of class
```

The first line in this section,

```
import java.io.*;
```

refers to a package of pre programmed routines supplied by the language. Java has many packages, containing a number of very useful routines. The packages are divided into areas of functionality and are extensively documented in the Java API listings which you bookmarked at the end of the last chapter. Each package contains classes and their methods; by importing them into our program, we can gain access to these methods and save ourselves the trouble of re-inventing the wheel. This particular package is called **java.io** and by adding the **.*** to it, we are saying that we want access to all the classes it contains. * is used as a wildcard, to indicate all or any.

Now let's examine the structure of the program.

There are two concepts fundamental to object oriented programming in Java, *objects* and *variables*:

• **Objects** contain methods and data which allow them to communicate with other objects and the system.

• **Variables** are defined as being of a certain data type, such as **char** (character) or **int** (integer), and contain values of that type. A variable may be found inside an object, or may be passed to an object in the form of an *argument*.

Since Java is an object oriented language, everything is defined as *classes*. When a class is compiled and run it becomes an *object* and exists in memory until the program ends, or until the program has no further use for it. In this simple example, we have only one class, which is defined within the lines

```
class MyFirst
{
    // class definition - variables and methods go here
}
```

This particular class has only one method which is called **main**, every java application must have a method called main, which can take parameters if required.

The definition of the method is given between the curly brackets. Notice the indenting of the brackets. This is not required by the compiler, but leaving one bracket out is probably the most common error in programming, and if you can see the pairs by scanning the page, it is easy to spot the missing one.

Finally the text contained between the /* and */ symbols is a *comment*. Comments are intended to preserve sanity, both yours and anyone who comes along and reads the code. You will find that if you come back to a long program after a month or two, you will have forgotten the thought processes that went into it. Comments are an excellent way of preserving these thoughts for future use. A single line comment is indicated by: //

```
// This is a single line comment
```

To summarise the story so far, if we want to write a program to print output to the screen, we need to go through these steps.

1. Identify the class and the packages you need to import from:

```
import java.io.*;

class MyFirst
{
}
```

2. Identify the classes' methods and insert them between the classes' containing brackets:

```
class MyFirst
{
    public static void main(String[ ] args)
    {
    }
}
```

3. Implement the methods:

```
class MyFirst
{
    public static void main(String[ ] args)
    {
        System.out.println ("Hello Birds, Hello Sky!!");
    }
}
```

4. Comment as required:

```
/* This is my first program. It is designed to
demonstrate a simple program structure
Author: Chris Wright 11.02.97 */

import java.io.*;

class MyFirst
{
    public static void main(String[ ] args)
    {
        System.out.println ("Hello Birds, Hello Sky!!");
    }
}
```

5. Compile
6. Correct if compilation is unsuccessful
7. Test (Run)
8. Correct if unsatisfactory

For a program of this size, it is appropriate to put the comments in last, when we start creating larger programs, we will comment as we go – with programming, we can never make life too easy!

—————— 2.3 Data types ——————

Java is a very strongly typed language, this means that when we want to store a value in memory we have to state a specific type. This helps the computer to allocate an appropriate amount of storage.

There are eight *primitive data types*, six numeric, one alphabetic and one Boolean.

The numeric types consist of:

- **int** which is the most commonly used, requiring 4 bytes of storage and covering whole numbers between –2,147,483,648 to +2,147,483,647

- **short** which uses half the storage (2 bytes) and covers numbers between –32,768 and +32,767

- **byte** which uses half as much storage as short (1 byte) and covers –128 to +127

- **long** which uses 8 bytes of storage and covers numbers between –9,223,372,036,854,775,808L and +9,223,372,036,854,775,807L

These integer types cover whole numbers only and are important for two reasons. They give us the opportunity to save memory requirements in large programs, giving us faster performance. Secondly, in Java, these ranges give us platform independence because they are known to work on all existing machines.

To store fractions we need two extra types:

- **float** which requires 4 bytes of storage and covers fractions with 7 significant digits.

- **double** which requires 8 bytes of storage and covers fractions with 15 significant digits.

Again the reason for having two types of fractions is for economy of storage.

The character type in Java is called:

- **char** which is used to contain single characters which are specified between single quotation marks ('Y' or 'N'). To contain longer sequences of characters we use an object called **String** which contains characters specified between double quotation marks ("Yes" or "No").

The last primitive data type is:

- **boolean** which contains the values *false* and *true*. This type is used for testing when there are only two possible outcomes.

2.4 Variables

To use the data types in a program, we need to explicitly declare a variable of a particular type. If, for example, we want to write a program to calculate my salary, we could declare a variable to contain its calculated value. We would do this by writing:

```
double mySalary;
```

Storage is usually declared at the top of a program, before the first method. Any data declared here will be accessible to all methods used by the class. Some methods require their own storage for temporary variables which are only of interest to that method. These may be declared in the same way, inside the method itself.

We can use any word for a variable, except for what are known as *reserved words*. These are words which are meaningful to the java compiler. There are 59 reserved words, including all of the data types. For a full list, see Appendix 1.

It is a good practice to choose composite, meaningful, words for variables, unless they are numbers used for controlling loops, (page 22) which are typically placed in variables *i*, *j* or *k*. The choice of name should help to make the program more readable.

If we needed more variables of the same type, we could write

```
double mySalary, myBaseSalary, myOverTime;
```

This would allow us to discover the value of our full salary by adding the value of the overtime to the base salary.

To compute the value of the overtime, we would need two more variables:

```
double hourlyRate;
int hours;                          // We will deal in whole hours
```

We now need to give the variable a value. We do this by a process known as assignment. To continue with the salary example, we would write:

```
myBaseSalary = 10000;        // Notice, no commas are used
hourlyRate = 5.50;
hours = 10;
```

Looking at the these declarations, it is easy to see that we can compute the value of the remaining variables by manipulating the ones we have assigned.

2.5 Operators

In Java the permissable operators are

+ Addition
– Subtraction
* Multiplication
/ Division
% Integer Remainder

To return once again to the Salary declarations, we can now manipulate the variables:

```
myOverTime = hourlyRate * hours;
mySalary = myBaseSalary + myOverTime;
```

In addition to these, we have *increment* operators (++) and *decrement* operators (– –) These are used to add 1 to or subtract 1 from the value of a variable. The use of these operators will be covered in the section on Control (see page 21).

You may be wondering how we can multiply a variable of type **float** by one of type **int**?

The answer is that Java assumes the answer to be in the larger type – in this case **float**.

This is true for the whole hierarchy of numeric types: e.g.

```
double * ( float, long, int, short, byte ) = double
float * ( long, int, short, byte ) = float
long * ( int, short, byte ) = long
int * ( short, byte ) = int
short * byte = short
```

This is fine, but what happens when we want the answer to be in the smaller type?

The answer is found in a process called *casting*. When casting down the hierarchy this has to be done explicitly:

```
double mySalary = 10000.65;
int approxSalary = ( int ) mySalary;
```

The value held in the variable approxSalary is 10000, note that the value is truncated, not rounded.

Relational and *Boolean* operators are used to compare values. The allowed operators are:

==	is equal to
!=	is not equal to
<	is less than
>	is more than
<=	is less than or equal to
>=	is greater than or equal to
&&	AND
||	OR

Armed with these operators, we can organise some conditional behaviour:

IF mySalary is less than myExpenses and myOverTime is equal to 0
THEN print "Bankruptcy Looms!"

This statement is in the form of *pseudocode*, a simple logical structure which is sometimes used to clarify matters before coding a complex problem. Before converting this into Java, we need to examine control structures.

——————— 2.6 Control structures ———————

This section describes the use of control structures in Java, much of which is logically identical to C and C++. Each subsection will show the control structure in the context of a program and explain any new features as they occur.

if.........*else*

If....else gives us a way of testing a statement. It has this format:

```
if( condition is true)
{
    do this;
    this;
}
else
{
    do this;
}
```

Here is an example of the **if...else** statement in use

```
import java.io.*;
class payCheck
{
    public static void main(String[ ] args)
    {
        double mySalary, myBaseSalary, myOverTime, hourlyRate;
        int hours;

        myBaseSalary = 10000;
        hourlyRate = 5.50;
        hours = 10;

        // we'll use a control structure
        // to check for overtime payments
        if (hours > 0)
            {
                myOverTime = hourlyRate * hours;
                mySalary = myBaseSalary + myOverTime;
            } // end if
        else
            {
                mySalary = myBaseSalary;
            } // end else

        /* Now print out the result - the value in mySalary is 'added'
           to the end of the message by the + sign  */
        System.out.println ("Your salary this week is £ " + mySalary);
    } // end method definition

} // Leave a space behind end class bracket so we can tell it apart
```

Notice that the condition upon which the first statement block is predicated is in brackets. The statement block can contain any number of statements. If the condition is not met, the program drops straight through to the **else** statement block.

Compile and run this program as it is written, then change the value of hours from 10 to 0 and compile and run it a second time. Try this for any other value of hours and watch the output change.

Note that it is not essential to have an **else** block. The simplest use of this structure is:

```
if (condition)
    {result if condition is true}
```

while

```
import java.io.*;

class MyFinance
{
    public static void main(String[ ] args)
    {
        // declare storage for variables
        double mySalary, myExpenses, myOverdraft, mySaving, surplus;

        int years;

        // initialise variables
        mySalary = 10000;
        myExpenses = 9500;
        myOverdraft = 20000;
        mySaving = 0;
        years = 0;

        // calculate a value for surplus
        surplus = mySalary - myExpenses;

        // test for the condition then execute block
        while (mySaving < myOverdraft)
            {
                // calculate a value of mySaving
                mySaving = mySaving + surplus;
                years++;             // add 1 to years
            }
```

```
    // print out the result
    System.out.println ("It is going to take you " + years +
        "years to pay off your overdraft!");
    }
}
```

There are a few new things to note in this program.

Firstly, the setting of variables to 0 at the top of the program. In the previous program, every variable has been allocated a value, either by initialisation at the top of the program, or by calculation within the program. In this program, if we look at the value of *mySaving*, we can see that it is used before it is given a value by the program. In these circumstances, we must always allocate the variable a value, otherwise the value will be whatever the computer finds in memory allocated to that variable, which could be left over from a previous program!

Secondly, if we examine the **while** statement, we can see that the program tests the condition before it processes the block. If the condition is not true, then the block will be ignored. Test this by allocating *mySaving* a value greater than the overdraft.

Thirdly, the line:

```
mySaving = mySaving + surplus;
```

may look a little strange if you are new to programming. What is happening here is that *mySaving* holds a value. If we want to change the value, it has to be reassigned. The simplest way to do this is to add our surplus for the year on to the original value.

do......while

If we need the program to execute a block of code at least once, we can use another construct, **do...while**:

```
do
    {
        mySaving = mySaving + surplus;
        year ++;
    }
while (mySaving < myOverdraft);
```

This sequence assumes that we do have an overdraft – the **while** condition checks at the end of the loop to see if the loop needs to be processed a second time.

for

With a **for** loop, we set the starting point and an end point and repeat the loop incrementing (or decrementing) until we hit the target. Logically we can shout 'Hurrah!' ten times by making it the action performed while we decrement a counter from 10 to 0 in the lines:

```
for (int i = 10; i=0; i--)
    {
        System.out.println("Hurrah! " + i + " Times!");
    }
```

This construct is used frequently in Java – it is amazing how many occasions require a counter!

```
import java.io.*;

class flatBroke
{
    public static void main(String[ ] args)
    {
        for (int i =10; i= 0; i-- )
        {
            System.out.println("Pounds left: £" + i );
        }  // end actions depending on counter
        System.out.println("Flat Broke!");
    } // end method

} // end class definition
```

switch

Java also supports a **switch** statement. This gives us a less cumbersome method of dealing with a range of possibilities than using a chain of **if** statements. The important thing to remember about the **switch** is that the data types it takes are restricted to **byte**, **char**, **short**, **int** and **long**. When using **double**, as in the example, we must cast the **double** to an **int** variable.

To return to the salary example

```java
import java.io.*;

class MyFinance
{
    public static void main(String[ ] args)
    {
        double mySalary, myExpenses, myOverdraft, mySaving, surplus;
        int years;

        mySalary = 10000;
        myExpenses = 9500;
        myOverdraft = 20000;
        mySaving = 0;
        years = 0;
        // calculate a value for surplus
        surplus = mySalary - myExpenses;
        // cast mySalary to int for switch statement
        int payCheck = (int)mySalary;

        // check salary and issue cautionary warning!
        switch (payCheck)
        {
            case 10000:        // same as if (payCheck == 10000)
            System.out.println ("One day you will earn more!");
            break;             // exit from switch structure
```

/* if paycheck was 1000 we need not continue, so break gets us
beyond the end of the switch statement, if not we try the next case
and so on until we satisfy the condition or use the default */

```java
            case 15000:        // same as if (payCheck == 15000)
            System.out.println ("15000 is not a bad salary...");
            break;

            case 20000:        // same as if (payCheck == 20000)
            System.out.println ("You shouldn't really have an
                overdraft!");
            break;

            default:       // handles all other values of payCheck
            // no default needed, we only need 3 messages
            break;
        } // end switch statement
```

```
    // test the condition then execute block
    while (mySaving < myOverdraft)
    {
        mySaving = mySaving + surplus;
        years++;
    } // end while

    // print out the result
    System.out.println ("It is going to take you " + years +
            " years to pay off your overdraft!");

    /* Note syntax in println - ("String " + variable + " String") allows
       us to add variable contents to the printed output */

    } // end method

} // end class definition
```

The **switch** statement here is used to output a message to the screen at particular points on a salary scale. If you change the variable *mySalary* to 10001, no message will be output. The program will drop straight through to the **default** behaviour (in this case none) and exit the **switch** statement.

An important feature of this structure is the use of **break** to exit. This can also be applied to the other control structures, to take into account special circumstances which would require a loop to terminate before it had met the condition.

break

The **break** statement is used at the end of each **case** block to exit from the **switch** structure. It may also be used as a way of giving two exit conditions for a loop. For example, in the program above, we may choose to break the loop if the number of years is greater than 100, as it is unlikely that we could pay off an overdraft over 100 years!

```
    // contained within method
    paymentPlan:
    while (mySaving < myOverdraft)
      {
        mySaving = mySaving + surplus;
        years++;
```

```
    if ( years >= 100 )
    {
        System.out.println ("Not in this lifetime!");
        break paymentPlan;
    } // end if
} // end while
System.out.println ("It is going to take you " + years +
    " years to pay off your overdraft!");
```

This example is called a *labelled break*. The label is
paymentPlan:, the effect of years reaching 100 will be to print
out the lines 'Not in this lifetime!' and 'It is going to take you 100
years to pay off your overdraft'.

If we omitted the label, only the **if** statement would terminate
and the program would continue calculating the exact number
of years it will take to reach solvency. The label must be placed
before the loop we want to break out of.

———————— 2.7 Methods ————————

So far, our classes have had only one method, *main*, and while
we are only creating simple programs, this is acceptable. As soon
as we introduce some complexity into a program, it becomes
difficult to visualise exactly what it is doing. Breaking the
responsibilities of a class into methods is beneficial because the
program becomes easier to understand and to visualise. In the
example below, we can follow the logic in the method *main*.

```
import java.io.*;

class methods
{
    public static void main(String[ ] args)
    {
        int number=4;                      // initialises the number to 4
        int answer=Square(number);         // calls the method Square
                                           // to deliver a value
        Display(answer);     // Displays the value found in answer
    }
```

```
public static int Square(int x)
// Takes an integer x as an argument
{
    return x*x;                    // returns the result as an integer
}
public static void Display(int a)
// Takes an integer and displays it
{
System.out.println("The answer is: " + a);
}
}
```

The declaration of the method

    public static int Square(int x)

means that the method is **public**, i.e. can be used by any object derived from this class. It is **static** to ensure that any of the class's other members can access it, without creating a separate instance of *methods*. It returns a value of type **int** and is passed a value of type **int**.

A method can be passed a variable to do some computing with, and can return a result. In this simple example, the line

    int answer=Square(number);

is the same as if we had written

    int answer=number * number;

By defining the calculation as a method, we gain the flexibility of being able to pass any number into it, at any point in our program, without worrying about how the calculation is done.

Part of the beauty of this approach is that it saves us from endless repetition. We will consider methods further in Chapter 3.

2.8 Arrays

An array is an example of a data structure. We can think of a simple one-dimensional array as a numbered list of variables of the same type. When we declare an array, we declare it as being of a data type, and then give it a variable name and a length:

```
String[ ] dinnerGuests = new String[8];
dinnerGuests[0] = "Fred";
dinnerGuests[1] = "Jane";
// repeat up to ...
dinnerGuests[7] = "Ruth";
```

You will notice that the first guest, Fred, is at position [0] in the array. Arrays in java run from 0 to (size – 1), in other words an array of 10 integers would consist of positions 0 to 9.

This initialisation of the array is a little long-winded for a large party, a shorter way would be to write:

```
String dinnerGuests[ ] = {"Fred", "Jane", "Michael", "Brenda",
"Chris", "Geraldine", "Gary", "Ruth"};
```

To access an element of an array, we refer to it by its index:

```
System.out.println(dinnerGuests[4] );
```

would print the name 'Brenda' to the screen.

By using a loop, we can print out all the names:

```
for (int i=0; i<=7; i++)
  {
   System.out.println("Guest number " + ( i + 1 ) + " is " +
   dinnerGuests[i]);
  }
```

2.9 Strings

Strings in Java are represented as a class, not as an array of characters. Because they are a class, they have methods such as **length()** and **substring()** which allow us to manipulate and compare them.

```
String virtue = "Good";
String sin = "Greed";

if (virtue == sin)
  {
    System.out.println("My name is Gordon Gecko!!");
  }
else
```

```
{
    System.out.println( virtue );
}
```

The code compares the two strings and hopefully finds that 'Greed' is not equal to 'Good'. It then prints 'Good' to the screen.

The method **length** gives us the length of a string as an integer.

```
int x = virtue.length( );
```

We can create new strings by taking a substring of an existing one.

```
String glue = virtue.substring(0, 3);
```

gives the new string glue a value of 'Goo'.

We can also alter an existing string by assigning it to itself:

```
String virtue=virtue.substring(0,3);
```

The string *virtue*, which contained a value of 'Good', now contains only 'Goo'.

—————— 2.10 Summary ——————

We now have the building blocks we need to create quite sophisticated programs. We have covered reserved words (see Appendix 1), and variable names, data types, the use and assignment of variables, operands and operators, the advantages of using methods, and the concept and practice of program control. We have also taken a brief look at Arrays and Strings.

All of the control structures we have used can be nested. This means that we can insert a while loop, for example, inside another control structure. This can be quite difficult to keep track of, so take care! At least one of the following exercises will require nested loops of some kind in order to reach an elegant solution.

We have also looked at good programming practice as we have moved through the chapter. Comments can be more useful than you might think at this stage, other good programming habits are the use of logical variable names, using white space to separate your blocks of code and indenting blocks so that you can easily see where one block ends and a new one begins. By paying attention to the way you lay out a program, you will save yourself hours of frustration – there is no sadder sight than a programmer unable to read their own program!

——————2.11 Common problems ———————

1. The file name must match the class name exactly.

2. Always check brackets exist in pairs.

3. All statements must be terminated by a semi-colon.

4. The correct command to run a program is **java myProg** not **java myProg.class**.

5. The quotes in **System.out.println("This variable contains " + x + "as a value");** bound the strings, not the **+ x +**.

—————— 2.12 Exercises ———————

1. Write a program to print five asterisks across the page.

2. Using a control structure, change the program to print a square made up of asterisks.

3. Modify this program to create a right angled triangle.

4. Write a program to create an equilateral triangle. (Hint: you can print blank spaces.)

5. Write a program to store three names in an array. If two of the names are identical the program should emit a warning – *'This password has already been chosen!'*

3
CLASSES AND OBJECTS

3.1 Aims of this chapter

Now that we have a firm grasp of control structures in simple programs, we need to start building some larger structures to see them in use. Everything we have done so far has included a line:

class ClassName

This line tells the compiler to create a class file called *ClassName.class*, or whatever name we decided to give the program. This chapter will explain the relationship between classes and objects; introduce encapsulation, composition and inheritance, and explain why these concepts are useful; and how we can use all this to build bigger and better programs. It will show how to design the most appropriate classes, how to create classes and how to use them.

This chapter will also take a look at the various packages of classes supplied with the JDK. One of the great strengths of Java is the abundance of reusable code which is supplied in the class libraries. Every time we use the line

import java.io.*

we have made available to our program all of the methods from the **java.io** class package. We will look at the available class packages and discover that reinventing the wheel is neither desirable nor necessary with object oriented programming.

—— 3.2 An object oriented program ——

What is an object? The classes that we have constructed so far are *definitions* of objects – the object does not exist until it is instantiated by running the code. So far we have used programs with only one class, so only one object has been created. However, the power of objects lies in the fact that they contain or encapsulate their own data and methods. The implication of this is that if we define one class and instantiate it several times, we get several different objects, each one with its own set of data and methods. If we designed a class to describe a bank account, we could use it many times to set up individual bank accounts. If we design code to describe an aeroplane, we can create an airforce! The following code is intended only as a demonstration of the power of object oriented programming, it is incomplete for simplicity's sake and exaggerated for clarity's sake!

```java
import java.awt.*;
import java.awt.image.*;

abstract class Aeroplane extends Object
// create aeroplane template – an  abstract class would never
// be instantiated, only used to derive specialised classes from.
{
   // give it some necessary data
   public int speed;
   public int height;
   public int engines;
   public int fuel;

   // tell it where it is on the screen
   int x, y;
   // construct an object
   Aeroplane( )
   {
      this.x = 100;
      this.y = 100;
   }

   public abstract void Draw(Graphics g, ImageObserver o);

   public void Fly( )
```

```
    {
       .......// as if by magic!
    }
} // end class definition

class Airliner extends Aeroplane
{
    public Airliner( )
    {
       super( );   // initialises the base class (Aeroplane) variables
       private int seats;
    }

    public void Draw(Graphics g, ImageObserver o);
    {
       // Graphics code goes here
    }
}   // ends class definition

class Fighter extends Aeroplane
{
    public Fighter( )
    {
       super( );
       private int guns;
    }

    public void Draw(Graphics g, ImageObserver o);
    {
       // Graphics code goes here
    }

} // ends class definition
```

This example demonstrates a way we might choose to implement
a number of different aeroplanes. We have chosen aeroplanes
because all aeroplanes have some things in common, this gives
us an opportunity to abstract those qualities that all aeroplanes
share and to use them as a template for building any type of
aeroplane, thus saving us the tedium of coding masses of identical
code for each type of aeroplane. The first class, **Aeroplane**, is
the one which contains the data and methods we can share
amongst all aeroplanes. Since it is only a template, we designate
it abstract. We will never directly instantiate an object of type

Aeroplane, only copy it into other objects. This technique is demonstrated in our second and third classes. The effect of:

class Airliner extends Aeroplane

is to give our class **Airliner** access to all the data and methods of our abstract class **Aeroplane**. This means that all we have to do is to give our new class the data that makes it different, i.e. the number of seats, and we have a fully functional airliner. Similarly the third class **Fighter** is given guns. It is important to note that **Fighter** would not get the extra seats, unless it extended **Airliner** instead of **Aeroplane**. The inheritance hierarchy in this case looks like this.

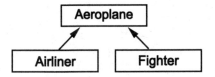

Inheritance from superclass Aeroplane

This is a very simplistic example of inheritance, and assumes a great deal – for instance where did the gun come from? How does the engine work? The answers to these questions requires a section to itself.

— 3.3 Introduction to object orientation —

In order to understand object orientation fully, it is necessary to take a step backwards and examine the history of software engineering and the way in which it is maturing as an industry.

Software engineering is a very youthful industry, and we have to look to other industries for possible reflections and clues as to what may happen in the future. If we look at the oldest industry of all, that of construction, we see an interesting phenomenon. That phenomenon is specialisation and it is this that enables us to erect structures such as St Paul's Cathedral from scratch, then to refine the techniques to build bigger and better versions.

If we look more closely at specialisation, we can see some ideas that we can use in software engineering. The point of a specialist is that they are the experts – all anyone else needs to know is where to find them and what they might expect them to do. Object orientation attempts to model this relationship. If we can use an existing class as a basis for another class, we only need to know where to find it, and what we can expect it to do. This is referred to as inheritance in software engineering, and designing classes to collaborate in this way is a highly valued skill. Inheritance is only one of three ways in which classes can be related.

We have looked at an example that models inheritance. This could be referred to as an IS A relationship – An Airliner IS A Aeroplane. There is another type of relationship that is not so simply modelled – HAS A. It would be unlikely that the good people at SunSoft have modelled classes to provide us with guns and engines for aeroplanes, and yet these are complex pieces, essential to an aeroplane's aeroplaneness. This relationship is termed *composition*. An aeroplane is composed of things of which it categorically is not an example. So an airliner IS A aeroplane and it HAS A engine. When designing class structures, it is important to get this relationship right in order to optimise the benefits of object orientation.

In the diagram below, we see that Object B, *Car.java* uses Object A, *Engine.java* as a component. Object C, *Turbo.java* inherits all the attributes of Object A, *Engine.java* and adds some more, such as fuel injection.

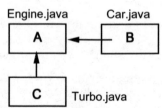

Object relationships - inheritance and composition

Having seen a skeleton of an inheritance model, we can look at the full code for a trivial example of object modelling using composition. Look out for the keyword **new** which indicates that we are creating an instance of the class **address**.

This is a working example, albeit trivial. The files can be compiled separately or together, but keep them in the same directory.

```
public class address
  {
   private String street;
   private String city;
   private String county;
   private String country;

   // established data storage, now construct class
   // passing it some values as parameters
   public address(String s, String c, String co, String cou)
   {
      street = s;
      city = c;
      county = co;
      country = cou;
   }

   // provide an accessor method to pass data with
   public String retrieve( )
   {
      return street + "," + city + "," + county + "," + country;
   }

} // end class definition

// This is the main class, which declares an instance of address
import java.io.* ;

public class Contact
{
   public static void main(String[ ] args)
   {
      String name = "Joe Soap";

      // create new object
      address a = new address( "10 Downing Street",
            "Westminster", "London", "England");
System.out.println("Name= " + name + " Address= "+ a.retrieve( ));
   }

}
```

It should be possible to see, from this trivial example, that a bigger application might be a Contact book, which could include classes for Name, Address and Telephone numbers. The general rule when designing classes is that if you have a large number of variables to deal with, and some of them are of the same category, such as the lines of an address, then you have a candidate for a further class. The advantages of this approach, which may not be immediately apparent in such a trivial example are that the details of the **address** class are hidden from the class that uses it. This means that if we decide to alter the way in which the display is put onto the screen, we know that all of the code that we need to alter will be found in one place – the **retrieve()** method of the **address** class – the internal details of the **retrieve()** method matter not a jot to the **Contact** class, so we need alter nothing else in the whole program. If for a moment we revert to our previous example of aeroplanes and engines, the benefit should be obvious; we have a single implementation of an engine which might be used by many different aeroplanes. By upgrading that one class, we immediately upgrade any object that is instantiated using that engine – i.e. the whole airforce!

The relationships between classes we have looked at so far include Composition and Inheritance. There are also circumstances where we would like different classes to behave in partially similar ways. In Java this is dealt with by the use of *Interfaces* (see page 74).

CLASS RELATIONSHIPS

Use – when a class uses the public methods of another class

Inheritance – when a class is derived from another class

Composition – when a class is composed of other classes

When we design an object oriented program, the first task is to identify the objects (classes), the second to identify the objects responsibilities (methods). A popular method to establish the beginnings of a class structure is to examine the problem analysis and isolate the nouns. These will often become classes. The verbs will often become methods. Looking at an analysis of an address book, we could say that:

My *address book* contains the *addresses* of my *Contacts*. I want to *add*, *alter* and occasionally *delete Contacts*. When I look up the name of *Contact* x, I would like the *book* to *retrieve* their *street*, the *town* and their *telephone number*.

From this simple description we can isolate three objects, **Contact**, **Book** and **Address**. We can assume that **add**, **alter**, **delete** and **look up** will be the responsibility (methods) of **Book**. The **street**, **town** and **telephone number** are data fields belonging to **Address**, so the **retrieve** method for these fields will be the responsibility of **Address**.

—————— 3.4 Inside objects ——————

Now that we have looked at the big picture, we should look in detail at the code we have used in our examples.

This class is very simple. It merely provides storage for the details of an address, which are passed to it when the class is constructed. It has only one method, which enables it to extract the details of the address from memory and return them as a String to the caller. Notice that the data declarations are given *visibility modifiers*. If a class is to be used with other classes, it is important that the visibility of methods and data is stated. This helps to maintain a consistent interface for other programmers to use.

```
public class address
{
    private String street;
    private String city;
    private String county;
    private String country;

    // established data storage, now construct class
```

The keyword **private**, used above defines the visibility of the data, as seen by other classes. There are three levels of visibility in common use: **private**, **protected** and **public**.

* **Private** means that no other class can directly manipulate the private data or method.

- **Protected** means that only classes derived from the class containing the protected data or methods can operate on them directly.

- **Public** means that any other class can manipulate the designated methods or data.

In practice it is customary to keep all data private to a class. This helps the programmer to maintain a consistent interface with other classes. In order to access this data, we provide a method called **display**, which returns the data as a String. This method is public, i.e. other classes can use this method. The important thing here is that the interface to this class is provided by the method – once the class is designed, all we need to know is that the address will be returned as a String. This gives us the freedom to modify the class in the future, without having to alter any other code in programs that use it.

It is important to remember that we have to explicitly declare the number and type of the arguments that are required by this class. We also have to explicitly allocate any argument passed to the class in its constructor method to memory, if we want to be able to access it from other methods. For convenience, we refer to the variables that are passed with different names. This reminds us that the arguments we have declared are method variables (**s**, **c**, **co** and **cou**), in order to use them elsewhere in the class, we must copy them to class variables (**street**, **city**, **county** and **country**).

```
public class address
{
    private String street;
    private String city;
    private String county;
    private String country;

    // having declared class variables, we can provide a constructor
    public address(String s, String c, String co, String cou)
    {
    // assign arguments to class variables, to access them later
        street = s;
        city = c;
```

```
        county = co;
        country = cou;
    }
    // class will be instantiated with suitable data when called
```

This part of the class is called a *constructor* method. We provide this method with a number of parameters, which in this case are the details of an address. These details are allocated storage in memory.

```
    // provide an accessor method to pass data with
    public String retrieve( )
    {
        return street + "," + city + "," + county + "," + country;
    }
} // end class definition
```

The last part of the class is an *accessor* method, which simply enables us to gain access to the data. Another type of method might be termed a '*mutator*' method, which would afford us a way of altering the data.

The next class is a class that is composed with the address class, in other words it HAS A address. Instead of a constructor method, we provide it with a *main* method which does all the processing needed.

```
public class Contact
{
    public static void main(String[ ] args)
    {
        String name = "Joe Soap";

        // create new object
        address a = new address("10 Downing Street",
                "Westminster", "London", "England");
        System.out.println("Name= " + name + " Address= "+
            a.retrieve());
    }
}
```

The code contained in the **main** method of class **Contact**, declares a String variable called **name** and creates an object of type **address**, passing to it the details it requires in its constructor method. By creating the class here with the keyword **new**, we automatically call the constructor method of that class. The next line is a call to **System**, to print out the contents of the variable **name**, and to use the **retrieve** method of our object **a**, in order to print the details of the address. Remember that until we create an instance of the class, the object does not exist, so we cannot call this method without first declaring a new variable of type **address**.

———— 3.5 Using class libraries ————

As we have already mentioned, one of the greatest strengths of Java lies in the extensive libraries. The most important libraries are the Abstract Windowing Toolkit (AWT) and the Net package which provides methods to make computer to computer connection possible. We will look in some detail at these in later chapters, but now is a good time to see how we can use methods provided by these packages to save needless hours of work. A full reference to the contents of these packages can be found at the Sun web site:

http://java.sun.com/products/jdk/1.1/docs/api/packages.html

This reference is a vital part of the programmer's armoury, so bookmark it immediately. Nearly all Java programs make use of the packages listed in the Java API (Application Programming Interface), so a complete reference to these packages is an invaluable guide.

The packages available to the programmer are these:

- **java.applet** Contains the Applet class which is the superclass of all applets (page 56).

- **java.awt** The Abstract Windowing Toolkit, contains classes in the categories of Graphics (for use with colours, fonts, images, etc.), Components (GUI components such as menus, buttons, lists, etc.) and Layout Managers which control the layout of components within their container objects (Chapter 6, 7 and 8).

- **java.awt.datatransfer** New in JDK1.1, supports inter application data transfer with cut and paste via Clipboard.

- **java.awt.event** New in JDK1.1, defines a new and improved way of dealing with events. Not yet supported by Netscape or Microsoft Explorer so restricted to applications (page 156).

- **java.awt.image** Classes for image manipulation (page 73).

- **java.awt.peer** Interface definitions, beyond the scope of this book.

- **java.beans** New in JDK1.1, contains the tools to allow programmers to make their own beans.

- **java.io** Contains classes to enable file creation by applications, and reading and writing to the screen (page 10).

- **java.lang** Contains integral objects such as String, class wrappers such as Boolean, Double, Integer and Throwable which is used in exception handling.

- **java.lang.reflect** New in JDK1.1, allows classes to inspect themselves via the Member Interface. Beyond the scope of this book.

- **java.math** New in JDK1.1, contains extra maths classes allowing arbitrary precision integer and floating point arithmetic.

- **java.net** Contains a powerful set of networking classes allowing access to URLs, and computer to computer communication (page 174).

- **java.text** New in JDK1.1, contains tools to implement internationalisation of code.

- **java.util** Contains utility classes such as vector and stack, date, hashtable which provide us with data structures useful to programmers (page 194).

- **java.util.zip** New in JDK1.1, contains data compression tools

To demonstrate the use of class libraries to its most dramatic effect, we need a project which requires a Windows-style interface and which we can continue to develop further on in the book.

The project is to build an interface to a game, which we will call Drag Racing. The game will consist of an animation which will take place in a frame. The user will be able to make bets on the outcome of each race. The components we would need for such an interface would be a button to start the race, an area to enter our bet, an area to view the accumulating losses and an area to post the name of the winning vehicle. It should look like this:

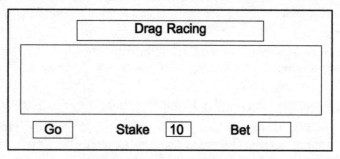

Rough design for drag racing game

Prior to applications such as Visual Basic, this interface would have taken many weeks to create. With judicious use of the AWT, this can now be reduced to minutes.

We have already used one Java package, **java.io** (page 11) in order to write to the screen, this program requires us to build a windows type interface. The package we require to do this is the **java.awt**, the first line in the example imports the package, allowing us to use library methods to build the interface.

We will be looking at the AWT in detail in a later chapter, so some of the code in the example may seem obscure. Briefly, we are using inheritance to give us access to the class Frame, which encapsulates a top-level application window. We can supply our own methods to look after event handling, and use a container class Panel, that is also provided by the AWT to hold our components. We can also use a class that implements LayoutManager to organise the components on the panel.

Events are the means by which Java handles actions. If the user enters a number, this is an Event and an Event Handler is written to deal with it. This is discussed in detail in Chapter 8.

```java
import java.awt.*;

public class Bets extends Frame
{
    Choice numbers;    // pull down menu to list the numbers
    TextField bet;     // holds the actual bet in integers

    public Bets( )                          // construct the object
    {
        numbers = new Choice( );       // initialise pull down menu
        numbers.addItem("1");
        numbers.addItem("2");
        numbers.addItem("3");
        numbers.addItem("4");
        numbers.addItem("5");

        bet = new TextField(2);   // initialise Text Field to hold 2 digits

        Panel p = new Panel( );  // initialise a panel to put things on
        p.setLayout(new FlowLayout( ));   // get a layout manager
        p.add(new Button("GO"));        // add a button to the panel
        p.add(new Label("Stake"));
        p.add(numbers);
        p.add(new Label("Bet"));
        p.add(bet);
        add("South", p);   // add panel and components at base
    }
    // we need a method to look after our choices
    public boolean action(Event e, Object o)
    {
        String result= null;
        if (e.target.equals(numbers))
        {
            result = Integer.toString(numbers.getSelectedIndex( )+1);
            bet.setText( result);
        }
        else if (o.equals("GO"))
        {
            start( );
        }
        return true;
    }
```

```
    public void start( )
    {
        // Insert code here to start race
    }
    // what happens if we close the window?
    public boolean handleEvent(Event e)
    {
      if (e.id == Event.WINDOW_DESTROY)
      // system event initiated by closing a window
          System.exit(0);
      else return super.handleEvent(e);
      return true;
    }
    public static void main(String[] args)
    {
      Frame f = new bets( );      // declare and initialise a Frame
      f.resize(300, 100);         // how big is it?
      f.show( );                  // wheel it on screen!
    }
  } // end class definition
```

The program when run, will produce this interface.

Simple interface created from AWT components

The point of this exercise is twofold, to introduce a game that we shall develop at various stages throughout the book, and to demonstrate the *use* of other objects in a programmer defined class. Every time you see the keyword **new** used in the example code, we are instantiating an object of a class found in the Java AWT package. Every component of this interface is found are in the Java AWT. We can use these objects by importing the package into the program with the statement

    import java.awt.*;

Golden rule. Always check the Java documentation to see if there is anything that will save you from doing any real work!

———— 3.6 Building your own classes ————

In this section, we will look at the process of designing our own classes, the decisions we make about what responsibilities a class should have, and how it will interact with other classes to give us a fully functioning program.

The example application we will examine is a mathematical calculator. The first thing to look at when designing classes is the verbal description of what the system is composed of. This should give us a first clue as to the identity of some of our classes.

System   - Calculator

Components   - Display
                      - Keypad

Functionality - Mathematics   - Add
                                          - Subtract
                                          - Multiply
                                          - Divide
                                          - Cancel

A calculator user interface

There are two obvious candidates for classes here, **Display** and **Keypad**. If we can create a generic display and a generic keypad, so that we can use them again for other programs, these are components in the truest sense of the word. It is obvious that there is no inheritance relationship here, nor is there a compositional relationship, yet it is equally obvious that these objects must know about one another in order to work together.

So we have two classes and two problems. How do the classes communicate? And where does the maths get processed?

The first question is the easiest one to answer. We can pass an object as a parameter to the initialisation method of a class – once it knows about the object it can send it messages. The second question is a little more complicated. We know that the keypad is a part of the overall graphical user interface, and we know that the mathematics will be done as a result of the keys being pressed. Why don't we bundle the mathematics with the keyboard? The answer is that if we were designing an applet, we probably would, but since we are designing an application, and since our company has also received orders for a set of burglar alarm interfaces, we would prefer to separate the functionality from the interface if possible.

To solve this problem we need to borrow a procedure from the realm of human computer interaction (HCI). This procedure is called *task analysis* and is concerned with isolating the components of a task in order that we can understand it better and build successful computer interfaces.

Let's begin by examining the sequence of events that occur when we use a calculator. (We assume that it is switched on.)

1. Enter a number – whole or decimal
2. Check that the number is displayed correctly
3. If it is, enter an operator
   Else If it isn't press cancel and return to 1.
4. Enter a second number
5. Check that it is displayed correctly
6. If it is, enter an equals sign
7. Read the result from the display.

This sequence actually gives us four clear indications of subtasks.

    Entering a number

    Cancelling a number

    Entering an operator

    Entering an equals sign

In each of the first two subtasks, the display is used as a value holder – this may seem obvious, but will be significant later.

Let's look again at the subtask *entering an operator*.

The number is on the screen. We check that it is the number we intended to type in and we press an operator button, or cancel it. If we cancel it, we don't need to store it anywhere, if we press an operator button, we do.

Do generic keypads have operator buttons?

If we separate the keypad from the operator pad we will have a truly generic keypad, that we could extend to become a burglar alarm pad. The keypad need only know about the display. Its area of responsibility is simply to write numbers onto a display, read numbers from it and cancel the wrong numbers.

The operators on the other hand define the mathematics. We can attach the mathematics to the operators, thus giving us a class that we can easily extend to give the calculator extra functionality. So we now have the possibility of using three classes to provide the GUI components and the functionality, **Display**, **Keypad** and **Maths**. We will also need a class to contain these components, one that we might call **Calculator**.

Lets look at the responsibilities of each class, and try to work out the methods they will need to be provided with.

The class **Calculator** merely needs to declare instances of the other classes and to provide the window in which the components will sit. It will also need to provide a handler for events occurring to that window.

A skeleton definition would include:

```
public class Calculator extends Frame
{
   // Construct object  here
   public Calculator( )
   {
      // Initialise objects and place on default panel
   }

   public boolean handleEvent(Event e)
   {
      // what happens when window is closed
   }

   public static void main(String[ ] args)
   {
      // Display top level window
   }
}
```

Now let's examine our class **Display**. This class needs to furnish a TextField and the ability to read and write data to and from it.

```
class Display extends Panel
{
   // construct class
   public Display( )
   {
      // initialise object and place on Panel
   }
   public void write(String s)
   {
      // write data  in the form of a string to the textField
   }

   public String read( )
   {
      // read data from the textfield
   }
}
```

That is as much as we need for the **Display** class – there is no data processing attached. What is significant is the fact that textfields can only read and write strings. This means that we have to think of a way of converting a number to a string and back again, if we are to do any mathematics in the **Maths** class.

Before we go to the **Maths** class, we still have one simple class to create, the **Keypad**.

```
class Keypad extends Panel
{
   Display monitor;
   // create class variable so we can access it later

   public Keypad(Display mymonitor)
   // Keypad needs to know about Display
   {
      monitor = mymonitor;              // initialise instance variable
      Panel p = new Panel( );
      // arrange a grid of 15 cells to hold buttons
      p.setLayout( new GridLayout(5,3));

      // Use loop to create 9 buttons
```

```java
    for ( int i = 0; i <= 9; i++)
       p.add(new Button("" + (char)('0' + i)));
    p.add(new Button("."));

    // use some blank buttons to balance display
    p.add(new Button(""));
    p.add(new Button(""));
    p.add(new Button(""));
    p.add(new Button("C"));

    add("Center", p);
}

public boolean action(Event e, Object o)
{
    /* switch will take a char, not a string. We can use a method
       from the string object to get the first (and only) char.*/
    char c = ((Button) e.target).getLabel( ).charAt(0);
    switch(c)
    {
        case '0':
        case '1':
        case '2':
        case '3':
        case '4':
        case '5':
        case '6':
        case '7':
        case '8':
        case '9':
        case '.':
            /* All we need to do here is to read the display and add
               the latest input to it.*/
            monitor.write(monitor.read( ) + c);
            break;  // if it is a digit or decimal point, exit switch

        case 'C':
            monitor.write("");   // overwrite wrong number with blank
            break;  // if it is C, exit switch and start again
    } // end switch
    return true;
} // end method
} // end class definition
```

Now we can turn our attention to the **Maths** class, this will be the object that actually does the processing. The **Maths** object needs to know about the **Monitor** object, but since we are using the TextField as a holder for our figures, it doesn't need to know directly about the **Keypad**.

```java
class Maths extends Panel
{
    Display monitor;

    private double num1, num2, result;
    private char operand;

    public Maths(Display mymonitor)
    {
        /* sets up operator keys and copies mymonitor to monitor
           - block works in the same way as the numeric keypad */
    }

    public boolean action(Event e, Object o)
    {
    char c = ((Button) e.target).getLabel( ).charAt(0);
    switch (c)
    {
        case '+':
        case '*':
        case '-':
        case '/':
            /* Assume the number is correct, so the consequence
            of pressing an operand is to place the number into our
            private variable, using another library routine to convert
            the string from monitor into a double.*/
            num1 = Double.valueOf(monitor.read( )).doubleValue( );

            operand = c;        // we also need to record the operator.....
            monitor.write("");      // ....and clear the textField.
            break;

        case '=':
            num2 = Double.valueOf(monitor.read( )).doubleValue( );
            // do the maths by calling a class method sum( )
            result = sum(num1, num2, operand);
            // write the answer to the display
            monitor.write(String.valueOf(result));
```

```
    }
    return true;
    }

    // And this is how the maths are done!
    public double sum(double x, double y, char z)
    {
        // initialise a variable to hold the answer
        double answer = 0;
        if (z == '+') answer = x + y;
        else if (z == '-') answer = x - y;
        else if (z == '*') answer = x * y;
        else if (z == '/') answer = x / y;
        return answer;
    }

} // end class
```

That is a bare bones implementation of our four classes. This is
not the only way to implement a calculator, but it is economical
and once the classes have been designed and we are clear about
which classes need to send messages to each other, then the
implementation is simple. Your task now is to fill in the missing
code from the class descriptions, or use the listing provided below.

```
import java.awt.*;

public class Calculator extends Frame
{
    Display out;
    Keypad in;
    Maths sums;

    public Calculator( )
    {
        setLayout(new BorderLayout( ));        // see Section 7.3

        out = new Display( );
        in = new Keypad(out);
        sums = new Maths(out);

        add("North", out);        // add at the top
        add("Center", in);        // add in the middle
        add("East", sums);        // add at the right
    }
```

```java
   public boolean handleEvent(Event e)
   {
      if (e.id == Event.WINDOW_DESTROY)
      System.exit(0);
      else return super.handleEvent(e);
      return true;
   }

   public static void main(String[] args)
   {
      Frame f = new calculator( );
      f.resize(100, 200);
      f.show( );
   }
}
class Display extends Panel
{
   TextField show;

   public Display( )
   {
      show = new TextField(10);
      Panel p = new Panel( );
      p.add(show);
      add ("Center", p);
   }

   public void write(String s)
   {
      show.setText(s);
   }

   public String read( )
   {
      return show.getText( );
   }
}
class Keypad extends Panel
{
   Display monitor;

   public Keypad(Display mymonitor)
   {
      monitor = mymonitor;
```

```
    Panel p = new Panel( );
    p.setLayout( new GridLayout(5,3));

    for ( int i = 0; i <= 9; i++)
        p.add(new Button("" + (char)('0' + i)));
    p.add(new Button("."));
    p.add(new Button(""));
    p.add(new Button(""));
    p.add(new Button(""));
    p.add(new Button("C"));

    add("Center", p);
    }

    public boolean action(Event e, Object o)
    {
    char c = ((Button) e.target).getLabel( ).charAt(0);
    switch(c)
    {
        case '0':
        case '1':
        case '2':
        case '3':
        case '4':
        case '5':
        case '6':
        case '7':
        case '8':
        case '9':
        case '.':
            monitor.write(monitor.read( ) + c);
            break;
        case 'C':
            monitor.write("");
            break;
    }
    return true;
    }
}

class Maths extends Panel
{
    Display monitor;
    double num1, num2, result;
    char operand;
```

```java
public Maths(Display mymonitor)
{
    monitor = mymonitor;
    Panel p = new Panel( );
    p.setLayout(new GridLayout(5,1));
    p.add(new Button("+"));
    p.add(new Button("-"));
    p.add(new Button("*"));
    p.add(new Button("/"));
    p.add(new Button("="));

    add("North",p);
}
public boolean action(Event e, Object o)
{
    char c = ((Button) e.target).getLabel( ).charAt(0);
    switch (c)
    {
        case '+':
        case '*':
        case '-':
        case '/':
            num1 = Double.valueOf(monitor.read( )).doubleValue();
            operand = c;
            monitor.write("");
            break;
        case '=':
            num2 = Double.valueOf(monitor.read( )).doubleValue();
            result = sum(num1, num2, operand);
            monitor.write(String.valueOf(result));
    }
    return true;
}
public double sum(double x, double y, char z)
{
    double answer = 0;
    if (z == '+') answer = x + y;
    else if (z == '-') answer = x - y;
    else if (z == '*') answer = x * y;
    else if (z == '/') answer = x / y;
    return answer;
}
}
```

3.7 Summary

In this chapter we have covered classes and objects, we have seen the three relationships that classes can have (use, composition and inheritance) and we have examined the issues surrounding visibility of data and methods used in classes. We have seen how messages can be sent to classes from other classes and we have been through the design cycle for a simple object oriented calculator. We have also looked briefly at the packages that are part of the Java API (Application Programming Interface) and we have learnt that life is too short to reinvent the wheel!

3.8 Exercises

1. Design, using inheritance, a class structure to hold details of all employees in a company.

2. Write a program to implement a burglar alarm, using the classes supplied with the calculator program. Your program should take input from a numerical keypad and check it against a known four-figure sequence. You should provide methods for the user to change the keycode and to display an 'ALARM' message when the code is entered wrongly.

3. Write a class called **currentAccount** that includes methods to deposit and withdraw money, and to inspect the balance. Make three instances of this class called *Fred*, *Jane* and *Tom*. Initialise them all with the same amount of money and withdraw different amounts from each account. Get the balance printed to the screen. What can you deduce from this exercise about the object in the computer's memory?

4

APPLETS

4.1 Aims of this chapter

The aim of this chapter is to start creating some real life programs and to display them in a Web browser. In the course of this chapter we will do more work with methods, learn how to pass values from one method to another and how to put a finished applet into a Web page using HTML tags. We will then move onto more advanced applets featuring simple animation and we will see how we can make our applets interactive.

4.2 Applets and applications

An *application* is a program that is installed on a network or personal computer and run from a command line or by clicking on an icon. The code for that program is resident on the computer or network responsible for running it. Applications are able to read and write files, print and have access to the hard drive and operating system of the computer that they are running on.

An applet is a program that runs within a Java-enabled Web browser such as Internet Explorer or Netscape. Usually, an applet will be resident on a remote server, and is called from within a Web page written in HTML. Because there is no way of knowing what applets are contained within a Web page, applets are not allowed to have access to the hard drive of a computer for security reasons. This means that an applet cannot invoke any other program, cannot directly save a file and cannot print. Imagine what the consequences might be if applets could read and write files – the details of your finances could be stolen, your files could be replaced by a malicious applet, or your computer could even be disabled. Because of these concerns, there are effectively two layers of protection from applets, firstly in the language itself – it is not possible to use certain features – and secondly the Java-enabled browsers impose their own restrictions on applets.

Inevitably, there are differences in the way that Netscape and Internet Explorer handle applets. These are hardly documented and therefore unpredictable. For this reason, it is essential to check that an applet does perform in the browser, before unleashing it onto the Internet.

An applet is derived from (extends, inherits) the **Applet** class, which is part of the **java.applet** package. The **applet** class is itself a subclass of **java.awt.Panel** so it provides a top level panel for us to arrange GUI components on (These terms were covered in Chapter 3).

At this time, the event handling mechanisms available to applets are only those from version 1.0. This is because the implementations of the Java Virtual Machine built into Web browsers have not yet been made version 1.1 compliant in all cases.

—————— 4.3 A first applet ——————

For a first applet, we will do a multimedia version of the old favourite, Hello World. This applet will display a picture instead of some text. To accomplish this, you will need a picture in GIF or JPEG format. It is useful to have a graphics workshop of some kind to look after file conversion. There are two that come very highly recommended: PaintShop Pro (http://www.jasc.com/) which is responsible for the images in this book and Graphic

Workshop for Windows (http://www.mindworkshop.com/alchemy/
alchemy.html). Both can be downloaded from the Internet.

To create an applet, we extend (make a subclass of)
java.applet.Applet. This class contains a number of methods
that are called automatically by the Web browser. These are:

init( ) initialises the applet

destroy( ) frees system resources when the applet is stopped

start( ) kicks off the real action of the applet

stop( ) pauses the applet's execution.

As Applet is subclassed from **Component**, via **Container** and
Panel – the **Component** method **paint( )** can be used to bring
graphic images to the screen. We would normally override at
least the **init( )** method of **java.applet.Applet**, because this is
the method that initialises all the variables and objects that the
applet requires.

Overriding means supplying a body to the method which is
different to the one provided by the Java library, or by the original
programmer. Essentially it gives us a means of customising a
class that is provided with a very basic behaviour pattern. The
example applet simply brings a graphic to the screen.

```
import java.applet.Applet;
import java.awt.*;        // we need the AWT to use the type Image

public class helloApplet extends Applet
{
    Image image;        // declare the picture, to be stored as an
                        // object of type Image

    public void init( )
    {
        /* The getImage function takes a URL and a filename as
        parameters. If we keep the image in the same directory
        as the class file, we need not supply a path. */
        image = getImage(getDocumentBase( ), "Jimmy.gif");
    }
    public void paint(Graphics g)
    {
        // Use a graphics object to render the image at position 1,1
```

```
      g.drawImage(image, 1, 1, this);
   }
   public void start( )
   {
      repaint( );
   }
}
```

The first thing you will notice about this code is that there is no **public static void main( )** statement. This is replaced in an applet by the **init( )** method, which initialises the applet, i.e. sets up the environment so that the processing can take place. Once the **init( )** method has been processed, the **start( )** method is called automatically. The call to **repaint( )** within **start( )** is the standard way to handle graphics in Java.

You can check that these automatic calls are occurring very easily, and this is an excellent way to debug programs that are not working as intended. Add a line to the import section:

```
   import java.io.*;
```

This allows you to print to a DOS window, while the applet is running in the AppletViewer. If you now add the line

```
   System.out.println("Start Method Called");
```

to the beginning of the **start( )** method's body, the message will be printed out in the DOS window as soon as the computer executes that line. You can use this technique to check the value of variables at various stages in your program if you are getting unexpected results.

```
   System.out.println("My variable x is: " + x + " at this point in the
   program")
```

Within **init( )**, the line:

```
   image = getImage(getDocumentBase( ), "Jimmy.gif");
```

uses the **getImage( )** method of the **Image** class in order to find the actual picture. The method takes an URL and a filename as arguments, here we are using the **getDocumentBase( )** method from **Applet** to get the location of the Web page containing the applet. If we keep the picture in the same directory as the class file, then we can refer to it directly.

The **paint( )** method renders the contents of image to the screen, by using the **drawImage( )** method from **Graphics**. **paint(Graphics g)** gives us access to the Graphics methods.

```
g.drawImage( image, 0, 0, this );
```

drawImage( ) takes four parameters: a reference to the picture to be drawn, x and y co-ordinates to position it within the applet area and a reference to an ImageObserver interface. This relays information about the status of the image to our program.

Before we can run this class, we need an HTML setting for it.

———— 4.4 Applets and HTML ————

Using the text editor, create a file called *Hello.html*, and save it to the same directory as your class and image. The file should contain the following text.

```
<HTML>
<BODY>
<APPLET CODE = "helloApplet.class" WIDTH =150 HEIGHT=150>
</APPLET>
This is the first applet in Teach Yourself Java
</BODY>
</HTML>
```

Having saved this file, you can view your applet by typing:

appletviewer Hello.html

at the command prompt.

You will probably find that it takes a second or two to render the image. We have used the Attributes WIDTH and HEIGHT, to tell the browser how much room to allow for the applet. There is also an ALIGN attribute that can be used to position the applet on the page, relative to the text that surrounds it.

ALIGN = LEFT would place the applet at the lefthand margin and following text would be displayed on the right of the applet. You can use another attribute HSPACE or VSPACE to specify a gap between the applet and the text.

<HTML>
<HEAD>
<TITLE>Here's Johnny!</TITLE>
<BODY BGCOLOR= "LIGHTBLUE">
<H3> Wrapping Text</H3>
The following applet is meant to illustrate the ability of HTML to
display applets within a prescribed area, keeping a set margin
between the applet and the text.
<APPLET CODE = "helloApplet.class" WIDTH =150 HEIGHT=250
ALIGN = LEFT VSPACE = 10 HSPACE=10>
</APPLET>
This is the first applet in Teach Yourself Java, while simple, it
allows us to experiment with the tags that control page positioning.
This text should wrap around the applet, leaving a 10 pixel gap
between text and the edge of the applet. If you want to change the
arrangement, go right ahead and experiment.
</BODY>
</HTML>

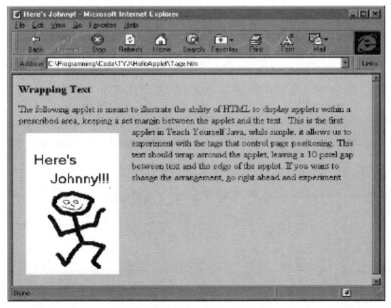

Displaying an applet with text

These are the other tags available with ALIGN

LEFT	Applet to left of page
RIGHT	Applet to right of page
BOTTOM	Bottom of applet in line with bottom of current line of text
TOP	Bottom of applet to top of current line of text
TEXTTOP	Top of applet to top of current line
MIDDLE	Middle of applet to base of current line
ABSMIDDLE	Middle of applet to middle of current line
BASELINE	Bottom of applet to baseline of current line
ABSBOTTOM	Bottom of applet to bottom of current line

You can also use the <APPLET> tag to pass parameters to an applet. This can be useful when you want to use a different font. For example, to make the Applet stand out from the rest of the text.

```
<APPLET CODE = "NewFont.class" WIDTH=150 HEIGHT=150>
<PARAM NAME=font VALUE="Courier">
</APPLET>
```

This parameter can be passed to the **paint( )** method of an applet by including the line

```
String fontChoice = getParameter("font");
```

then set the font with

```
Font f = new Font(fontChoice, Font.BOLD, 25);
g.setFont(f);
```

and use it

```
g.drawString("This Font is large and looks like a typewriter!");
```

4.5 More applets

We have just seen how we can put graphics into pages. Now we will look at Text and Fields.

The applet we are going to write is a simple temperature converter. The applet will contain two fields and two text Labels describing them.

Centigrade/Fahrenheit conversion applet

The first thing to know about Fields is that they are a class belonging to the AWT package, so we need a line at the beginning of the program to **import java.awt.*;** . The second thing is that there is no equivalent number field. All numbers are treated as text if they are displayed in a Field. This means that we have to explicitly convert them in both directions. Fortunately Java supplies us with library routines to do this.

```
Integer.parseInt(TextFieldName.getText( ));
```

reads text and converts it to an integer value,

```
TextFieldName.setText(Integer.toString(f));
```

places an integer **f** into a TextField as a piece of text.

We need the compulsory **init( )** method to put the text and Fields on the screen, an **action( )** method to read text from the Centigrade field and write it to the Fahrenheit field and a **calc()** method to do the conversion.

We need to declare all our variables at the top of the program before we write any code. In this program we need two objects of type **TextField**, two objects of type **Label** to hold the description or instructions, and three **integers**, two to hold the Centigrade and Fahrenheit values and one to hold the result after the calculation has been done.

The first part of the program will look like this:

```
public class TempCon extends Applet
{
   Label CentLabel, FarLabel;
   TextField Centin, Farout;
   int f, c, answer;
```

```
public void init( )
{
    CentLabel = new Label("Please enter the Temperature in
        degrees Centigrade");
    Centin = new TextField(5);

    FarLabel = new Label("Temperature in degrees Fahrenheit is:");
    Farout = new TextField(5);

    add(CentLabel);
    add(Centin);
    add(FarLabel);
    add(Farout);
}
```

Notice that after we have declared that we are going to use these Label and TextField classes, we have to explicitly instantiate them in the **init( )** method. When we instantiate the objects, we can give them some information. The **Label** object needs to know the Text, which is passed to it as a **String** and therefore needs to be contained within quotation marks. The **TextField** needs to know how much text is expected to display, so we give it an integer argument enumerating the number of characters. After we have done this, we add the objects to the applet.

The next problem, is how to deal with the input. For this, we will use an event handling method called **action( )**. This method takes an Event and an Object as arguments. The action method is actually provided by the **Component** class, by supplying our own version of what we expect to happen, we are overriding the method, or changing its functionality. **action( )** returns a boolean value, *true* or *false*. If it returns *true*, then we are saying that we have handled the event, if it returns *false*, the event would be passed up the hierarchy of classes until it is handled. In practice, it is our business to see that all events are handled. In this case the event is caused by the user hitting the 'Enter' key on the keyboard after they have entered the number. All we need to do is supply code to handle this event, and return *true* to notify the program that we have handled it.

When we receive the keyboard event, we need to read the text from the textField, convert it to a number, call our **calc( )** method to perform some number crunching on it and write the result back to the screen, as text.

```
public boolean action(Event e, Object o)
{
    c = Integer.parseInt(Centin.getText( ));
    f = calc(c);    // places the value returned by calc( ) into f
    Farout.setText(Integer.toString(f));
    return true;
}
```

The last thing we should examine is the **calc( )** method.

```
public int calc(int x)
{
    answer=(((9 * x)/5) + 32);
    return answer;
}
```

The first line tells us that this is a public method, that it returns an integer value and that it takes an integer as an argument. The body of the code consists of the algorithm for converting Centigrade into Fahrenheit. Notice that in the method header, the argument is specified as **int**eger **x**, not **c**. This is because we are describing a *type* of variable, not a specific instance of one. When the method is called as **f = calc(c)** the compiler checks that **c** is an integer, similarly the return type must match the receiver **f**. Here is the complete code.

```
import java.applet.Applet;
import java.awt.*;

public class TempCon extends Applet
{
    Label CentLabel, FarLabel;
    TextField Centin, Farout;
    int f, c, answer;

    public void init( )
    {
        CentLabel = new Label("Please enter the Temperature in
                    degrees Centigrade");
        Centin = new TextField (5);
        FarLabel = new Label("Temperature in degrees Fahrenheit is:");
        Farout = new TextField(5);
```

```
    add(CentLabel);
    add(Centin);
    add(FarLabel);
    add(Farout);
}

public int calc(int x)
{
    answer=(((9 * x)/5) + 32);
    return answer;
}

public boolean action(Event e, Object o)
{
    c = Integer.parseInt(Centin.getText( ));
    f = calc(c);
    Farout.setText(Integer.toString(f));
    return true;
}
} // end class definition
```

————4.6 An interactive applet————

The magic ingredient that Java offers to Web designers is interactivity. For our next applet we will return to the racing game, and design a way of placing bets on the outcome of the race. The rules are quite straightforward, the user starts with a pot of money, say £100, and places a bet on the outcome of the race. If the chosen car wins, the game adds a sum equal to the bet, to the pot. If the chosen car loses, the game keeps the bet. When the user has no more money left, or presses the QUIT button, the game ends.

We have not written any animation code yet – that will be coming up in the graphics section, so we will place bets on the outcome of a randomly generated number between 1 and 4. The user chooses a number, and if the computer's choice matches it, the user wins.

The first thing to do is to declare the class variables. We need integer storage to hold the bet, the amount of money we have left in the pot, the amount of money the house has left (the bank) and the actual result of the race. We also need to store the objects we are importing from the AWT, so every textField, Label and Button will be declared here.

```
import java.awt.*;
import java.util.*;      // to handle our text to integer conversions
import java.applet.Applet;

public class Betting extends Applet
{
    private int bet, pot, bank, car, result;
    private Label betLabel, potLabel, bankLabel, carLabel;
    private TextField betField, carField, potField, bankField,
winnerField;
    private Button goButton;

    public void init( )
    {
    }
}
```

We now need to fill in the public method **init( )**, so that everything shows up on the screen.

```
public void init( )
{
    betLabel = new Label("Enter Bet");
    carLabel = new Label("Choose Car");
    potLabel = new Label("Pot");
    bankLabel = new Label("Bank");

    betField = new TextField(5);       // size of field in characters
    carField = new TextField(2);
    potField = new TextField(5);
    bankField = new TextField(7);
    winnerField = new TextField(20);

    potField.setEditable(false);
    bankField.setEditable(false);

    goButton = new Button("Start Race");

    add(goButton);
    add(betLabel);
    add(betField);
```

```
     add(carLabel);
     add(carField);
     add(potLabel);
     add(potField);
     add(bankLabel);
     add(bankField);
     add(winnerField);

     betField.setText("");
     potField.setText("100");          // size of pot in cash
     bankField.setText("1000");        // size of bank in cash
}
```

Now that we have an interface, we need to know how to play the game. Remember that the idea is to add this interface to a much larger program, so we need to make it as generic as possible.

We will need are an event handling method – **action( )** to start the race via a push button, and a method to give us a result – we will call this **Race( )** (When we implement the game proper, this method will be replaced). The important thing is that **Race( )** should return an integer, as that will give us something to compare to our predicted winner. We will need to check if we have won or not. The method **isWinner( )** will take the actual result, compare it with our prediction and return a boolean value *true* or *false*. Depending on this, will be the **play( )** method which will read in the data, set the game off, wait for the result to be returned and administer winnings or, more likely, losses. The first thing to look at is our race method. In this context, all **Race( )** needs to do is to return a randomly chosen number, restricted from a choice of 4. We can do this by using the **Math.random( )** method from **java.util** – a technique that may come in useful later.

```
public int Race( )
{
    int z;
    z = 1 + (int) (Math.random( ) * 4);
    return z;
}
```

Math.random( ) returns a double between 0.0 and 1.0. Here we multiply it by 4, then cast the result to an integer and add 1, as we do not have a car 0. This gives us a range between 1 and 4.

Our method to determine the winner is equally simple. When called, we give it the result of the race and our prediction as parameters and simply compare the two.

```
public boolean isWinner(int x, int y)
{
    if ( x == y)
    return true;
    else
    return false;
}
```

The **action( )** method will start the game

```
public boolean action(Event e, Object o)
{
    if (e.target == goButton)
        play( );
    return true;
}
```

The last method **play( )** is where the logic of the game resides. To define this method, we can analyse the task of playing the game. Remembering that the game may be played several times by one user, the first thing to do is to clear the text from the winnerField. Now, for the sake of simplicity, we store the bets and state of our finances in the appropriate variables, by converting the text values to integers as we did with the calculator.

Next we get the result of the race by calling **Race( )**, and print it out in the textField to avoid arguments later! All that remains is to administer the money, by subtracting the bet from the pot if we have lost, and adding it to the bank, or vice versa in the unusual event that we win.

```
public void play( )
{
    winnerField.setText("");
    bet = Integer.parseInt(betField.getText( ));
    pot = Integer.parseInt(potField.getText( ));
    bank = Integer.parseInt(bankField.getText( ));
    car = Integer.parseInt(carField.getText( ));
```

```
      result = Race( );
      winnerField.setText("Winner is " + Integer.toString( result));

      if (isWinner(car, result) == true)
      {
         pot = pot + bet;
         potField.setText( Integer.toString(pot));
         bank = bank - bet;
         bankField.setText( Integer.toString(bank));
      }
      else
      {
         pot = pot - bet;
         potField.setText(Integer.toString(pot));
         bank = bank + bet;
         bankField.setText(Integer.toString(bank));
      }
   }
}
```

Here is the interface in Applet Viewer, followed by the code for the complete program. Try altering the program so that it checks to see if either the user or the bank has no money left, and so that instead of inputting the number of the car, we select it from a pull down menu.

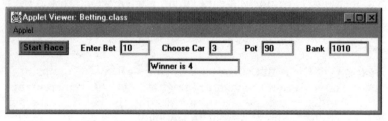

User interface for betting game

```
import java.awt.*;
import java.util.*;
import java.applet.Applet;

public class Betting extends Applet
{
   private int bet, pot, bank, car, result;
   private Label betLabel, potLabel, bankLabel, carLabel;
```

```
private TextField betField, carField, potField, bankField, winnerField;
private Button goButton;

public void init( )
{
   betLabel = new Label("Enter Bet");
   carLabel = new Label( "Choose Car");
   potLabel = new Label("Pot");
   bankLabel = new Label("Bank");

   betField = new TextField(5);
   carField = new TextField(2);
   potField = new TextField(5);
   bankField = new TextField(7);
   winnerField = new TextField(20);

   potField.setEditable(false);
   bankField.setEditable(false);

   goButton = new Button("Start Race");

   add(goButton);
   add(betLabel);
   add(betField);
   add(carLabel);
   add(carField);
   add(potLabel);
   add(potField);
   add(bankLabel);
   add(bankField);
   add(winnerField);

   betField.setText("");
   potField.setText("100");
   bankField.setText("1000");
}

public boolean isWinner(int x, int y)
{
   if ( x == y)
      return true;
   else
      return false;
}
```

```java
public int Race( )
{
   int z;

   z = 1 + (int) (Math.random( ) * 4);
   return z;
}
public boolean action(Event e, Object o)
{
   if (e.target == goButton)
   play( );
   return true;
}
public void play( )
{
   winnerField.setText("");
   bet = Integer.parseInt(betField.getText( ));
   pot = Integer.parseInt(potField.getText( ));
   bank = Integer.parseInt(bankField.getText( ));
   car = Integer.parseInt(carField.getText( ));

   result = Race( );
   winnerField.setText("Winner is " + Integer.toString( result));

   if (isWinner(car, result) == true)
   {
      pot = pot + bet;
      potField.setText(Integer.toString(pot));
      bank = bank - bet;
      bankField.setText(Integer.toString(bank));
   }
   else
   {
      pot = pot - bet;
      potField.setText(Integer.toString(pot));
      bank = bank + bet;
      bankField.setText(Integer.toString(bank));
   } // end else
} // end method

} // end class definition
```

——————4.7 Simple animation——————

As we have already seen, loading a graphic into an applet is not terribly hard. The next task is to try our hand at an animation. This will introduce us to several techniques that are used extensively in graphics programming. For this animation we are going to try and emulate a children's book style animation, where a figure is drawn with a slight difference on successive pages and the user flicks through the book in order to create the illusion of movement.

The first thing you need to do is to prepare twenty different small images. Start with one, and call it *filename0.gif*. The actual name is unimportant, but try and use something descriptive, and append a zero to the filename. Now alter it very slightly and save it as *filename1.gif*. Keep doing this until you have twenty one images, numbered 0 – 20. Save these images into the same directory as your class files.

Now we can start the programming part. This should be simple. In theory all we need to do is to run a loop which will increment the picture number and render it to the screen.

```
import java.applet.Applet;
import java.awt.*;

public class SimpleAnimation extends Applet
{
    private Image images[ ];
    private int frames = 20;

    public void init( )
    {
        images = new Image[frames];

        for (int i = 0; i < frames; i++)
        {
        images[i] = getImage(getDocumentBase( ), "Smile" + i + ".gif");
        }
    }

    public void paint(Graphics g)
    {
```

```
        for (int i = 0; i < frames; i++)
        {
            g.drawImage(images[i], 1, 1, this);
        }
    }
    public void start( )
    {
        repaint( );
    }
}
```

Try running this in appletviewer – it looks terrible doesn't it! The image flickers badly while loading and on occasions it doesn't load at all. There are two problems. Firstly, unless you have a very slow processor indeed, the frames cycle through in a second. Secondly the frames are not drawn fully to the screen, which gives the animation a jumpy, fractured look. The first thing we could do to solve this problem is to try and delay the second loop. This would allow us to create a presentation or slide show.

—————— 4.8 Slide shows ——————

To slow the applet down, we will need to create a separate *thread of execution*. A *Thread* is a path of execution through a program This applet is not truly multithreaded, but we need to set up a single different thread in order to slow the main program down. This is a very common use of threads – setting up timers to control the rate of execution of a program. We have a choice about how we implement a thread. We can use the **Thread** class, extend it to suit our purposes and compose our program using our improved version, or we can invoke the **Runnable** interface which allows us to use a **run( )** method to control the applet. With applets this is the more common solution as it cuts down on the number of classes used and therefore on the number of HTTP calls to the server.

Implementing an interface is a convenient way of borrowing the behaviour of an object without actually using inheritance. An interface to a class is a collection of methods that we must implement if we choose to use this technique. **Runnable** includes just one method, **run( )** which is automatically passed to the **Thread** class.

```java
import java.applet.Applet;
import java.awt.*;

public class SimpleAnimation extends Applet implements Runnable
{
    private Thread animate;      // declare a Thread
    private Image images[ ];
    private int frames = 20;
    private int count = 0;

    public void init( )
    {
        // load all the images
        images = new Image[frames];

        for (int i = 0; i < frames; i++)
        {
        images[i] = getImage(getDocumentBase( ), "Smile" + i + ".gif");
        }
    }

    public void paint(Graphics g)
    {
        g.drawImage(images[count++], 1, 1, this);
        // this refers to an instance of SimpleAnimation
        if (count == frames)
        count = 0;
    }

    public void start( )
    {
        if (animate == null)
        {
            animate = new Thread(this);  // initialise a thread
            animate.start( );            // starts thread running - calls run( )
        }
    }

    public void stop( )
    {
```

```
    if (animate != null)
    {
    animate.stop( );            // pause thread
    animate = null;             // free up resources
    }
}

public void run( )
{
    while (isActive( ))         // while there is a live thread
    {
    try                         // loop through this sequence
    {
       repaint( );
       Thread.sleep(1000);  // pause the thread 1 second
    }
    catch (InterruptedException e)
    {
    }

       animate = null;
    } // end while
} // end method

  } // end class definition
```

When using threads, it is important to realise that the
relationship between **start()**, **run()** and **stop()** is implicit. **run()**
is called automatically by **start( )**. **stop( )** is called when the
applet is closed. The use of the keyword **this** in the declaration
of the thread refers to an instance of the class SimpleAnimation
and ensures that the methods called are the ones we have defined
as methods of SimpleAnimation and not the default methods
supplied by the Thread class.

---------------- **4.9 Summary** ----------------

In this chapter we have learnt the difference between applets
and applications and looked at the implications in the short term
for use of JDK 1.1. We have written applets which display

graphics, and manipulate figures and while doing this have looked in greater detail at the techniques covered in earlier chapters, being put to use. We have looked at the use of multiple methods to break a task down into easy to code chunks, notably the use of the **calc( )** method in the temperature conversion program and **isWinner( )** in the betting game.

In addition we have touched on areas that we will be covering in later chapters, most notably Graphics and Threads. We have demonstrated that a graphic file can be loaded from a remote server and displayed in the graphics context of an applet. We have also learnt how to set up a simple thread so that the main program can control the rate at which the calls to **paint( )** are made.

——————— 4.10 Exercises ———————

1. Rewrite the Bets program to include methods for preventing the user from betting more funds than he has available.

2. Add a function to return the square of a given number to the calculator program.

3. Revise the slideshow applet to include a pause button which pauses at one click and releases on the second. (HINT – You will need to set a state for the button in the **action( )** method.)

4. Revise the slideshow to pause on a single mouse click. You will need to consult the Java API or Mouse Events (page 164) in order to discover how to do this.

5

SIMPLE GRAPHICS

5.1 Aims of this chapter

The aims of this chapter are to build up an understanding of how Computers use coordinates on the screen to position components, to write programs that create graphics primitives using the Java.awt and to gain an understanding of the role of **paint( )**, **update( )** and **repaint( )** methods in getting graphics to the screen.

We will examine colour, fonts and shapes and look at ways that we can control the presentation of text within an applet.

Finally we will be looking at more advanced graphics techniques such as buffering and clipping, used for smooth animation, and the use of MediaTracker to monitor the loading of separate image files into an applet.

redo

5.2 A first graphics program

In this program, we will see how the computer uses x and y coordinates to position components on the screen.

A computer screen is composed of pixels. The number depends upon the resolutions, but typically a display will be set to 800 by

600 pixels. The top left-hand corner is given the coordinates 0,0. Within this, each **Component** we draw also has its own coordinates, also starting at 0,0 at the top left. This gives us the ability to create complex graphical user interfaces by nesting components within one another.

This applet will follow the mouse around the screen and print out the coordinates in the status bar of your browser.

```
import java.awt.*;
import java.applet.Applet;

public class coordinates extends Applet
{
    private int lastX, lastY;
    private Color myColor = Color.blue;        // see page 81
    // Color not Colour – Java is American

    // set up background colour
    public void init( )
    {
        this.setBackground(Color.white);
    }

    // catch the mouse event to get first coordinates
    public boolean mouseDown(Event e, int x, int y)
    {
        lastX = x;
        lastY = y;
        return true;
    }

    // now draw a line from last coordinates to current ones
    public boolean mouseDrag(Event e, int x, int y)
    {
        Graphics g = getGraphics( );
        g.setColor(myColor);
        g.drawLine(lastX, lastY, x, y);
        lastX = x;
        lastY = y;
        showStatus("Mouse is at: " + lastX + "," + lastY);
        return true;
    }
}
```

This is an extremely basic drawing applet. We get the first set of coordinates from the initial **mouseDown** action, then as we drag the mouse around the screen, the coordinates are constantly updated and joined together. There is no call to **paint( )** in this applet, because we do not want to update the screen. If we did we would lose the drawing!

5.3 Fonts

Our next applet will demonstrate drawing text to the screen, in different fonts, colours and sizes. As with previous applets, the first thing we do is to declare our data – here we are going to use a series of String objects which can be declared and initialised at one go. We are also going to call on the **Graphics.Font** class to give us some control over what the text will look like.

```
import java.awt.*;
import java.applet.Applet;

public class Fonts extends Applet
{
    private String s1 = "This is an Helvetica Font Size 16, Italic";
    private String s2 = "This is Times New Roman Size 12, Bold";
    private String s3 = "This is Courier Size 20";
    private Font f1, f2, f3;
```

Because we are using coloured fonts, it would be nice to set the background to some other colour, so that the colours will show up nicely. This is always done in the **init( )** method. We also define our Fonts in the **init( )** method. A Font definition takes three arguments, a String describing the name of the Font, a call to the Font class to determine the presentation style (This is always done in capital letters BOLD, ITALIC or PLAIN), and finally a point size integer which maps exactly onto the point sizes used in word processing.

```
    public void init( )
    {
        setBackground(Color.black);
        f1 = new Font("Helvetica", Font.ITALIC, 16);
```

```
        f2 = new Font("TimesRoman", Font.BOLD, 12);
        f3 = new Font("Courier", Font.PLAIN, 18);
    }
```

Now that we have set the applet up, all that remains is to draw the text to the screen. This is done via a call to **Graphics**. In this case, since we are using different colors and fonts, we need three calls to Graphics for each line, one to set the color, one to set the font and another to draw the string. The call to **Graphics.setColor** takes the color constant available to Color as an argument. **Graphics.setFont** takes our pre-defined Font style as an argument and **Graphics.drawString** takes the pre-defined String and the X and Y coordinates that determine its position on the applet.

```
    public void paint(Graphics g)
    {
        g.setColor(Color.red);
        g.setFont(f1);
        g.drawString(s1, 20, 20);

        g.setColor(Color.pink);
        g.setFont(f2);
        g.drawString(s2, 20, 50);

        g.setColor(Color.yellow);
        g.setFont(f3);
        g.drawString(s3, 20, 80);
    }

} // end class definition
```

There are also graphics methods available to check what fonts are available, what font is being used and the size of the font being used. The next applet will demonstrate the use of these methods and the use of the **FontMetrics** class to get more detailed information about fonts.

The **FontMetrics** class gives us six methods for obtaining information about a font. These include:

getFont( )   returns a Font object
getFontList( )   returns a list of available fonts

getAscent( ) returns the height in points of the highest letter
getDescent( ) returns the depth the font requires below the baseline
getLeading( ) returns the leading – the distance between lines
getHeight( ) returns the height of a font.

The **FontMetrics** class is not derived from **Font**, but from **Object**. This means that when we use it, we use it with the current **Graphics** object, rather than the current **Font** object.

```
import java.awt.*;
import java.applet.Applet;

public class Fonts1 extends Applet
{
   private String s = "What are the details of this Font?";

   private Font f;

   public void init( )
   {
      setBackground(Color.black);
      f = new Font("TimesRoman", Font.ITALIC, 20);
   }

   public void paint (Graphics g)
   {
      int style, size;
      String s1, s2, s3, s4, s5, s6, s7, name;

      g.setColor(Color.red);
      g.setFont(f);
      g.drawString(s, 20, 20);

      name = f.getName( );
      s1 = name;

      style = f.getStyle( );
      if (style == Font.PLAIN)
         s2 = "Plain";
      else if (style == Font.BOLD)
         s2 = "Bold";
      else if (style == Font.ITALIC)
         s2 = "Italic";
      else s2 = "";
```

```
        size = f.getSize( );
        s3 = size + "point ";

        g.drawString(s1, 20, 50);
        g.drawString(s2, 20, 70);
        g.drawString(s3, 20, 90);

        g.drawString("Font family is " + f.getFamily( ), 20, 110);

        int ascent = g.getFontMetrics( ).getAscent( );
        int descent = g.getFontMetrics( ).getDescent( );
        int height = g.getFontMetrics( ).getHeight( );
        int leading = g.getFontMetrics( ).getLeading( );

        s4 = "Ascent of Font = " + String.valueOf(ascent);
        s5 = "Descent of Font = " + String.valueOf(descent);
        s6 = "Height of Font = " + String.valueOf(height);
        s7 = "Leading of Font = " + String.valueOf(leading);

        g.drawString(s4, 20, 140);
        g.drawString(s5, 20, 170);
        g.drawString(s6, 20, 200);
        g.drawString(s7, 20, 230);
    }
}
```

These methods on their own, are fairly unspectacular, however they are useful for animation, in ways that will be demonstrated at the end of the chapter.

5.4 Colors

All colours are created from an RGB value. Java expresses RGB values as three integers in the range of 0 – 255. These control the amounts of Red, Green and Blue that make up the colour. The colour methods are defined in the **Color** class and include:

getRed( )	returns the R value
getGreen( )	returns the Green value
getBlue( )	returns the Blue value
getColor( )	returns a color object representing the current color
setColor(Color c)	sets the colour to be used by Graphics objects

```java
import java.awt.*;
import java.applet.Applet;

public class Colour extends Applet
{
    private Color c1, c2;
    private String s, s1, s2, s3, s4, s5, s6;

    public void init( )
    {
        c1 = Color.blue;
        c2 = Color.yellow;
        s = "This colour shows up fine against a blue background!";
        setBackground(c1);
    }

    public void paint(Graphics g)
    {
        g.setColor(c2);
        g.drawString( s, 20, 100);

        s1 = String.valueOf(c2.getRed( ));
        s2 = String.valueOf(c2.getGreen( ));
        s3 = String.valueOf(c2.getBlue( ));
        s4 = String.valueOf(c1.getRed( ));
        s5 = String.valueOf(c1.getGreen( ));
        s6 = String.valueOf(c1.getBlue( ));

        g.drawString( "Current text colour is RGB(" + s1+ "," +
            s2 + "," + s3 + ")", 20, 140);
        g.drawString( "Current background colour is RGB(" + s4+
            "," + s5+ ","+ s6+ ")" ,20, 170);
    }
} // end class definition
```

5.5 Shapes

The Java AWT provides a number of graphics primitives that can be used to create basic shapes. These primitives can be used via methods of the Graphics class. The first primitive is a line.

```java
import java.awt.*;
import java.applet.Applet;

public class Line extends Applet
{
   Color c , bc;

   public void init( )
   {
     bc = Color.black;
     c = Color.white;
     setBackground(bc);
   }

   public void paint(Graphics g)
   {
     g.setColor(c);
     g.drawLine(20, 20, 100, 100);
   }

   public void start( )
   {
     repaint( );
   }
}
```

This program simply makes the background black, sets the graphics colour to white and draws a line from 20, 20 to 100, 100 using the **Graphics.drawLine( )** method If we want to do anything more interesting with lines, we have to use rectangles with a bit of imagination. In the following program, we will draw a rectangle with a frame around it, a rectangle with a 3D frame and a rectangle that floats above the page. The four coordinates given to a rectangle give the starting point, a width and a height. These are the methods available to draw right-angled rectangles.

```
drawRect(x, y, width, height)
fillRect(x, y, width, height)
draw3DRect(x, y, width, height, true/false)
fill3DRect(x, y, width, height, true/false)
```

Notice the boolean in the 3D Rectangle – *true* indicates that the rectangle should be raised, *false* indicates that the rectangle should be sunken.

(x,y)

height

Drawing a rectangle

width

g.drawRect(x,y,width,height)

```java
import java.awt.*;
import java.applet.Applet;

public class rectangle extends Applet
{
    Color c, c2, bc;
    public void init( )
    {
        bc = Color.black;
        c = Color.white;
        c2 = Color.red;
        setBackground(bc);
    }

    public void paint(Graphics g)
    {
        // filled rectangle with a frame
        g.setColor(c);
        g.drawRect(20, 20, 100, 50);
        g.fillRect(25, 25, 90, 40);

        // filled rectangle with 3D frame
        g.setColor(c2);
        g.fill3DRect(100, 100, 80, 130, true);
        g.fill3DRect(102, 102, 76, 126, false);

        // Floating rectangle
        g.setColor(c2);
        g.fill3DRect(200, 200, 100, 150, false);
        g.fill3DRect(198, 198, 96,  146, true);
    }

    public void start( )
    {
        repaint( );
    }
}
```

We can use similar methods to draw rounded rectangles, again four parameters are required, and again they represent a starting point, a width and a height.

Here is the **paint( )** method of a program to draw rounded rectangles. The rest of the program is identical to the one above.

```
public void paint(Graphics g)
{
    g.setColor(c);
    // draw rounded rectangle
    g.drawRoundRect(20, 20, 50, 50, 10, 20);

    g.setColor(c2);
    // draw curvier rectangle
    g.fillRoundRect(100, 100, 80, 130, 50, 50);

    g.setColor(c2);
    // draw square
    g.drawRoundRect(200, 200, 100, 130, 0, 0);

    //draw circle
    g.fillRoundRect(300, 300, 80, 80, 80, 80);
}
```

You will notice that the method **drawRoundRect()** takes two extra arguments, these dictate the height and width of the curved area at the corner.

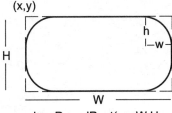

A rounded rectangle   g.drawRoundRect(x,y,W,H,w,h)

Methods available to draw rounded rectangles are

```
drawRoundRect(x, y, W, H, w, h)
fillRoundRect(x, y, W, H, w, h)
```

As we have observed in the previous applet, a curved rectangle can be manipulated to form a circle, by making the width and height of the curved area equal to half the width and height of the rectangle. A separate method exists to draw ovals. To predict where an oval will be drawn, imagine it is inside the smallest possible rectangle that would enclose it. The starting point is the top left-hand corner of the rectangle, which is actually outside the oval. The oval only touches the sides of the rectangle at mid point.

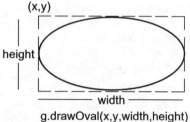

Drawing an oval g.drawOval(x,y,width,height)

Methods available to draw ovals are

    drawOval(x, y, width, height)
    fillOval(x, y, width, height)

Here is the **paint( )** method required to draw arcs. Notice that a filled arc fills the 'slice' between the arc and the centre of the bounding rectangle. An ordinary arc is also drawn relative to the rectangle's centre. To illustrate this, the arc in the following program is drawn inside a rectangle which has the same starting point.

```
public void paint(Graphics g)
{
    g.setColor(c2);
    g.drawRect(100, 100, 150, 100);
    g.setColor(c);
    g.fillArc(100, 100, 150, 100, 35, -130);
}
```

Notice that an arc takes six arguments. These represent the starting point, the width and height of the bounding rectangle, the starting angle measured from zero degrees at compass point east in an anticlockwise direction, and the angle of the arc, measured from the starting point to the end point. The minus sign in the last argument indicates that we want the arc to sweep in a clockwise direction.

Methods available to draw arcs are:

```
g.drawArc(x, y, w, h, start, finish);
g.fillArc(x, y, w, h, start, finish);
```

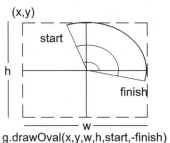

Drawing an arc　　　g.drawOval(x,y,w,h,start,-finish)

Polygons may also be drawn in Java. These are slightly more complicated because their nature is not fixed. A polygon can have any number of sides, so our job is to define the points that make up the beginning and end of each side, and then join them together. The **drawPolygon( )** method takes as arguments two arrays of integers containing the x and y coordinates and a single integer declaring the number of sides. The last set of coordinates should be the same as the first set – if you want the polygon to be closed. Java does not assume that all polygons are closed, so the number of points should be one more than the number of sides.

```java
import java.awt.*;
import java.applet.Applet;
import java.awt.Polygon;

public class TestPolygon extends Applet
{
    private int xCoords[ ] = {20, 100, 250, 140, 20};
    private int yCoords[ ] = {20, 100, 180, 75, 20};
    private Polygon p;

    public void init()
    {
        p = new Polygon(xCoords, yCoords, 5);
    }
    public void paint(Graphics g)
    {
        g.drawPolygon(p);
    }
}
```

This is not the only way to declare and draw a polygon, another method allows us to add the points individually as pairs of x and y coordinates;

```java
import java.awt.*;
import java.applet.Applet;

public class Test1Polygon extends Applet
{
    private Polygon p;
    public void init( )
    {
        p = new Polygon();

        p.addPoint(20, 20);
        p.addPoint(100, 100);
        p.addPoint(250, 180);
        p.addPoint(140, 75);
        p.addPoint(20, 20);
    }
    public void paint(Graphics g)
    {
        g.fillPolygon(p);
    }
}
```

Methods available to draw Polygons are

```java
g.drawPolygon(xCoords, yCoords, numPoints)
g.fillPolygon(xCoords, yCoords, numPoints)
g.drawPolygon(p)
g.fillPolygon(p)
```

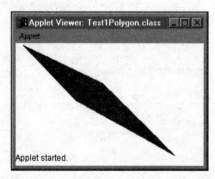

Drawing a polygon

—— 5.6 paint(), repaint() and update() ——

We have looked in some detail at ways of drawing text and images onto an applet. We have used **paint( )** to draw the desired shapes to the screen, and we know that applets inherit from **Component**. This is not the whole story. The inheritance chain that ends in an applet that we write begins at **java.lang.Object**, the base class for all classes in Java. The whole chain is represented below.

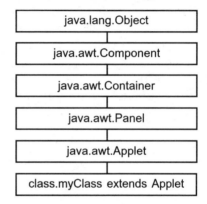

The inheritance chain leading to Applet

java.lang.Object
java.awt.Component
java.awt.Container
java.awt.Panel
java.awt.Applet
class.myClass extends Applet

The fact that our applet is the last in a chain, means that we can take advantage of many of the properties of classes above us. The fact that **Applet** is an extension of **Panel** means that the applet itself provides an area upon which we can draw. By importing **java.awt.*** into the program, we can use methods from anywhere in the AWT to manipulate this graphics area.

paint( ), **repaint( )** and **update( )** are methods belonging to the **Component** class of the AWT. They take as an argument, an object of type **Graphics** which represents the context in which the applet does its drawing. The **Graphics** class supplies the methods that we have used in this chapter to draw text and images and to set the paint mode.

The way that the drawing reaches the screen, is via the **paint( )** method of **Component**. However, when a window is open on a screen we cannot control what happens to it. It may be resized by the user, another window may be opened on top of it, or it may be moved. These events are beyond our control, yet amazingly the window remains intact. The reason for this is the **update( )** method of **Component**. This is called automatically when any of these events occur – its default implementation is to erase the background and call the **paint( )** method. Since our drawing code is usually in the **paint( )** method, this is adequate behaviour for most circumstances. It may be necessary with some programs to override the default implementation and provide a different sequence of actions for **update( )**. For example, if we are rebuilding a static image, it is obviously not necessary to erase the background, since it can be used again.

Another rendering method associated with component is **repaint( )**. This method in its default form sends a request to the AWT to call the components **update( )** method as soon as possible (thus ultimately calling **paint( )**).

There are four ways that **repaint( )** can be called.

repaint( )	Calls update( ) asap.
repaint(long t)	Calls update( ) in t milliseconds
repaint(x, y, w, h)	Calls update( ) but repaints only the rectangle (x, y, w, h)
repaint(long t, x, y, w, h)	Calls update( ) and repaints the rectangle (x, y, w, h) in t milliseconds.

————— 5.7 Graphics modes —————

Graphics modes dictate how graphics are drawn on the screen. If you alter one of the example programs to have the computer draw overlapping shapes, you will notice that the first shape is partially obscured by the second. This is the default graphics mode, known as *overwrite* mode. The other Graphics mode is called *XOR*, and its effect is that all the overlapped shapes can still be seen. To invoke XOR mode, we use the Graphics method **setXORMode(Color c)**. The colour that is used as an argument to **setXORMode( )**, dictates the colour of the overlapped area, and where both shapes are of the same colour, the overlapping area will be set to this colour. Where they are different colours, this colour is used to find a 'balancing' colour.

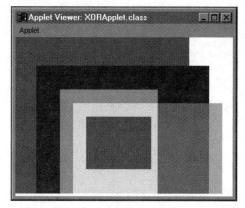

XOR Mode graphics

Here is the code used to generate this picture.

```java
import java.awt.*;
import java.applet.Applet;

public class XORApplet extends Applet
{
    Color c1, c2, c3, c4;

    public void init( )
    {
        c1 = Color.red;
        c2 = Color.blue;
        c3 = Color.green;
        c4 = Color.yellow;
    }

    public void paint(Graphics g)
    {
        g.setColor(c1);
        g.fillRect(0, 0, 300, 400);
        g.setColor(c2);
        g.fillRect(50, 50, 300, 400);
        g.setColor(c3);
        g.fillRect(100, 100, 150, 200);
        g.setXORMode(c4);
        g.fillRect(120, 120, 250, 300);
```

```
    g.setColor(c1);
    g.fillRect(140, 140, 100, 100);
  }
}
```

Notice that the fourth overlapping rectangle has its mode set to *XOR*. The result of this is that the overlapping areas are represented in different colours. The last rectangle is painted in *overwrite* mode and therefore appears in its own colour, even though it overlaps another rectangle.

—————5.8 Graphics techniques—————

In this section, we will look at some common graphics techniques that are used to provide flicker-free rendering of animations to the screen. These techniques include the use of Threads to slow an animation down, the use of ImageObserver to load images, use of clipping to minimise the redrawn area and buffering to smooth the passage of pictures to the screen.

Threads

A Thread refers to a sequence of operations forming a discrete task. In a multitasking operating system, we have an opportunity to organise concurrent processing of many tasks in order to increase the speed and efficiency of the program. Normally this is transparent to the user – it simply allows the computer to process some part of a program in the background, or to run multiple instances of the same class. The use of Threads in programming is exactly analogous to multitasking in an operating system. It is a very useful technique in the writing of user interfaces, because we can convey to the user the impression that their input is being processed immediately by putting the user I/O in a separate thread. The alternative, which will be familiar to people used to 16 bit operating systems such as Windows 3.1, is that the user has to wait until the program has finished the last task, before the program will accept input from the screen. This is frustrating at best.

The use of Threads in Java is therefore not restricted to graphics programs, but is used extensively in communications programming, for example. However the technique can be used to control animations very effectively.

The major problem with computer animation is that the progress of the animation has to be controlled by some sort of timer. If we use a simple looping structure, a modern processor will go through the loop so fast that the effect is lost. It takes rather more processing power to paint a graphic to the screen than it does to read through a sequence of integers. The effect is that the count has progressed before the computer has had time to draw the picture. By using a Thread, we can slow the process down to a reasonable speed, thus allowing a smoother operation.

Let's examine the example we used at the end of Chapter 4 to run a slide show. If we add some debugging code into it, so that we can see what's causing the problems, we should be able to solve them. (Extra code is shown in italics.)

```java
import java.applet.Applet;
import java.awt.*;
import java.io.*;

public class Smile extends Applet implements Runnable
{
    private Thread animate;    // declare a Thread
    private Image images[ ];
    private int frames = 20;
    private int count = 0;

    public void init( )
    {
        images = new Image[frames];

        for (int i = 0; i < frames; i++)
        {
         images[i] = getImage(getDocumentBase( ), "Smile" + i + ".gif");
        }
    }

    public void paint(Graphics g)
    {
        g.drawImage( images[count++], 1, 1, this);
```

```java
      System.out.println(" painting image: " +  count);
      if (count == frames)
      count = 0;
   }

   public void start( )
   {
      if (animate == null)
      {
         animate = new Thread(this);  // initialise a thread
         animate.start( );
         System.out.println("New Thread starting.....");
      }
   }

   public void stop( )
   {
      if (animate != null)
      {
      animate.stop( );
      animate = null;
      }
   }

   public void run( )
   {
      while (isActive( ))
      {
      try
      {
         System.out.println("Thread calling paint");
         repaint( );
         Thread.sleep(1000);  // pause thread for 1000 milliseconds
      }
      catch (InterruptedException e)
      {
         System.out("Exception: "+ e.getMessage( ));
      }

         animate = null;
      } // end while
   } // end method
} // end class definition
```

The first thing to notice is that the thread starts on schedule. Next, we see that the computer runs throught the whole list of pictures before we get a second call to **paint( )**. This is not what we expected to happen at all. The whole point of the thread was to increment one image at a time. Why should this be happening?

The answer is that our **paint( )** method contains this line:

```
g.drawImage(images[count++], 1, 1, this);
```

The last argument being passed to **drawImage** is a reference to this applet object. This call is actually to the **ImageObserver** interface which comes from the **Component** class, of which **Applet** is a direct descendant. The effect of **ImageObserver** is to automatically call **repaint( )** if the picture is not available when requested. Because we are incrementing *count* in the same line, **repaint( )** will cycle through the whole catalogue. So we should remove the increment and the testing for the *count* equalling the number of frames and place them in the run section of the thread. That way **ImageObserver** will recall **paint( )** on the same picture, until it is complete. If we compile and run the program again, we see that it cycles through much as before, except that it loads the images one at a time, instead of every image every time. On the second pass, the animation begins to behave in a more sensible fashion. Is there a way we can cut out the first pass through the image list?

MediaTracker

We could check that all the pictures are fully loaded by using a **MediaTracker** object, which we will call 'cache'. This would delay the **paint( )** method until all the images are checked. The extra code is in italics. First we declare the MediaTracker object 'cache', then, when we load the pictures into the images array, we register them with 'cache':

```
cache.addImage(pictures[i], i);
```

The second argument to **cache.addImage** sets a flag or signal that can be checked later. It is convenient to use the picture number, so that we can identify a particular picture if we have a runtime problem.

```
import java.applet.Applet;
import java.io.*;
import java.awt.*;

public class Smile extends Applet implements Runnable
{
    private Thread animate;
    private Image images[ ];
    private int frames = 20;
    private int count = 0;
    MediaTracker cache;

    public void init( )
    {
        frames = 20;
        count = 0;
        images = new Image[frames];
        cache = new MediaTracker(this);
        for ( int i = 0; i < frames; i++)
        {
        images[i] = getImage(getDocumentBase( ), "Smile" + i + ".gif");
            cache.addImage(pictures[i], i);
        }
    }

    public void paint(Graphics g)
    {
        g.drawImage(images[count], 1, 1, this);
        if (count == frames) count = 0;
        System.out.println("Picture " + count + " painted");
    }

    public void start( )
    {
        if (animate == null)
        {
            animate = new Thread(this);
            timer.start( );
        }
    }

    public void run( )
    {
        for (int i=0; i < frames; i++)
```

```
    {
    System.out.println("Loading Image: Smile" + i);
    try
    {
        cache.waitForID(i);
    }
    catch ( InterruptedException e)
        {
            System.out("Exception: "+ e.getMessage( ));
        }
    if (cache.isErrorID(i))
    {
        System.out.println("Error loading Smile" + i);
        return;
    }
    } // end for
    while (isActive( ))
    {
        try
    {
        System.out.println("Calling paint....");
        repaint( );
        count++;
        if (count==frames)
        {
            count = 0;
        }
        Thread.sleep(1000);
    }
        catch (Exception e)
        {
            System.out("Exception: " + e.getMessage( ));
        }
    } // end while
    animate = null;
    } // end run( ) method
} // end class
```

The code in the **run()** method does the same job as before, but
before it does that, we want to force the program to check that
all our pictures have been loaded.

```
    for (int i=0; i < frames; i++)
    {
        // print what's happening to System window
        System.out.println("Loading Image: Smile" + i);
        try
        {
        // check ID of each picture as loop increments
        cache.waitForID(i);
        }
        catch (InterruptedException e)
        {
            System.out("Exception: " + e.getMessage( ));
        }
        if (cache.isErrorID(i))
        {
        // If any picture is not loaded then let us know
        System.out.println("Error loading Smile" + i );
        return;
        }
    }
```

This section of code cycles through the MediaTracker object cache and checks that the flag is set correctly. If a picture were unavailable for any reason, this section would throw an exception. The **try .... catch** sequence allows us to put code in place to deal with a problem that may occur during file transfer – if we are dealing with an Internet download. This type of exception is possible, but unlikely on a standalone PC. We can proceed by checking for a particular ID and printing a warning message if we find it. The empty braces immediately after the **catch(InterruptedException e)** would contain code for dealing with an InterruptedException.

Running this program, the improvement should be radical. There is still a problem with the first picture, and a slight flicker when the image changes. For this we need a technique called *double buffering*.

There are three types of method used with MediaTracker objects: one to *register* the picture, four to *load* the picture and two to *check* that the picture is loaded. The first type of method, to register the picture can be used in two forms:

AddImage(Image im, int x)
Registers the image *im* and associates it with a number.

AddImage(Image im, int x, int w, int h)
Registers an image to scale (width, height) and associates it with a number.

Loading the picture can be accomplished in four ways:

checkAll(true)	Starts loading and returns immediately.
checkID(int x, true)	Starts loading all images associated with integer *x* and returns immediately.
waitForAll( )	Returns after the images are loaded
waitForID(int x)	Loads images associated with integer *x* and returns when finished.

The two methods used to check for errors in loading are:

isErrorAny( )	Returns true if errors occurred
isErrorID(int x)	Returns true if errors were encountered with images associated with integer *x*.

Double buffering

Double buffering is a technique used to eliminate flicker in animations. In simple terms, we get the computer to render the graphics in an offscreen buffer, before transferring them to the screen. This means that the picture is transferred whole to the screen rather than built up on the screen. The program is developed from the previous program. These are the parts containing changed or extra code.

```
public class Smile extends Applet implements Runnable
{
    int count, frames;
    Image pictures[ ];
    Thread timer;
    MediaTracker cache;
    Image offscreen;
    Graphics buffer;

    public void init( )
    {
        frames = 20;
```

```
      count = 0;
      pictures = new Image[frames];
      cache = new MediaTracker(this);

      offscreen = this.createImage(100, 100);
      buffer = offscreen.getGraphics( );

      for (int i = 0; i < frames; i++)
      {
      pictures[i] = getImage(getDocumentBase( ), "Smile" + i + ".gif");
      cache.addImage(pictures[i], i);
      }
   }
```

We declare an object of type **Image**, that we call *offscreen*. This will be used as a graphics context, matching the width and height of the onscreen drawing area. In order to draw it to the screen, we need to pass it to a **Graphics** object which we will call *buffer*. We can copy it to buffer using the **getGraphics( )** method.

```
  public void paint(Graphics g)
  {
      buffer.setColor(Color.white);
      buffer.fillRect(1, 1, 100, 100);
      buffer.drawImage(pictures[count], 1, 1, this);
      System.out.println("Printing smile" + count + " to the buffer");
      g.drawImage(offscreen, 1, 1, this);
      System.out.println("printing buffer to the screen");

      if (count == frames)
      count = 0;
  }
```

The **paint( )** method is now changed. We have a four-step process. First we set the colour of the buffer to white, and draw a rectangle, in order to clear the contents. We then draw the picture to the buffer instead of to the screen. Finally we move the contents of the buffer to the screen. The **System.out** lines are there to help see what is going on, but when the program is ready to be unleashed on the Internet, they can all be removed. It may still be a good idea to print a message to the browser's status bar, using **showStatus( )**, to reassure the user that something is happening, while the pictures are loading.

You may be wondering why we bother to change the background of the buffer to white. Since **repaint( )** is called in the **run( )** section, surely the background will be erased anyway, by the implicit call to **update( )**? This is true except that **update( )** will not clear the buffer's background, only the onscreen background. To prevent the same job being performed twice, we can override **update( )**, by including a rewritten version in our code.

```
update(Graphics g)
{
   paint(g);
}
```

This has the effect of restricting **update( )** to calling **paint( )**. Since we are explicitly clearing the old image from the buffer by drawing a white rectangle there, the effect is to reduce the work done by the processor.

Clipping

Clipping is a technique that is used to simplify moving an image across a static background. If the background does not change during the course of an animation, there is little point in drawing it every time we move a foreground object. This technique specifies an area that needs to be redrawn, which logically will include the area just vacated and the new area that is moved to. This is computed by measuring a rectangle around the moving picture and redrawing the union of position A and position B.

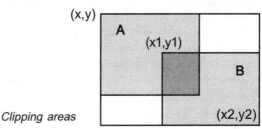

Clipping areas

In the diagram, the rectangle placed at (x, y) is moving to a new position at (x1, y1). The union of both positions will be bounded by the area starting at (x, y) with an opposite corner at (x2, y2).

The example below, bounces a line of text up and down the screen. Where it passes across a colour, you will notice that the colour is replaced as the text passes across it. Where the text moves across an area without an image, there is nothing to redraw so the text remains. Notice in this applet that we use the **FontMetrics( )** method to find out how big the rectangle should be that includes all the text.

The line:

```
Rectangle current = new Rectangle(x, y-sascent, swidth, sheight)
```

measures the current position of the string, using the variables *sascent*, *swidth* and *sheight*, We use *sascent* to ensure that we have no trail left by tall letters, remember that *y* increments downwards, so if we subtract the ascent from *y* we give ourselves headroom for the 't' and the 'h' in our string. We initialise these variables using **FontMetrics( )** like this.

```
FontMetrics fm = this.getFontMetrics(f);
swidth = fm.stringWidth(s);
sheight = fm.getHeight( );
sascent = fm.getAscent( );
```

This is the complete code.

```
import java.awt.*;
import java.applet.Applet;

public class BounceText extends Applet implements Runnable
{
    private int YIncr;
    private String s;
    int swidth, sheight, sascent;

    private int x, y;
    Color c1, c2, c3, c4, c5, c6;
    Font f;
    Thread animator;

    public void init( )
    {
        s = "Watch this Groooovy movie";
        x = 10;
        y = 20;
```

```
   c1 = Color.red;
   c2 = Color.blue;
   c3 = Color.green;
   c4 = Color.yellow;

   f = new Font("TimesRoman", Font.BOLD, 30);

   FontMetrics fm = this.getFontMetrics(f);
   swidth = fm.stringWidth(s);
   sheight = fm.getHeight( );
   sascent = fm.getAscent( );
}

public void start( )
{
   animator = new Thread(this);
   animator.start( );
}

public void stop( )
{
   if (animator != null)
      animator.stop( );
   animator = null;
}

public void drawBack(Graphics g)
{
   g.setColor(c1);
   g.fillRect(0, 0, 300, 400);
   g.setColor(c2);
   g.fillRect(50, 50, 300, 400);
   g.setColor(c3);
   g.fill3DRect(100, 100, 300, 400, true);
}

public void paint(Graphics g)
{
   drawBack(g);
   g.setColor(c4);
   g.setFont(f);
   g.drawString(s, x, y);
}
```

```java
public void run( )
{
    while (true)
    {
    // get area of applet to use in movement algorithm
    Dimension d = this.size( );

    Rectangle current = new Rectangle(x, y-sascent, swidth, sheight);
    // test for top of bounce area
    if (y <= 20)
    {
        YIncr = 2;
    }
    if (y > d.height)
    {
        // when it gets to the bottom, send it up again!
        YIncr = -YIncr;
    }
    y = y + YIncr;
    // now calculate new rectangle
    Rectangle next = new Rectangle(x, y-sascent, swidth, sheight);
    // obtain union
    Rectangle r = next.union(current);
    Graphics g = getGraphics( );

    // repaint only the union area
    g.clipRect(r.x, r.y, r.width, r.height);
    paint(g);

    try
    {
        Thread.sleep(100);
    }
    catch(InterruptedException e)
        {
            System.out("Exception: " + e.getMessage( ));
        }
    } // end while
    } // end method
} // end class
```

Notice the line:

```java
g.clipRect(r.x, r.y, r.width, r.height);
```

This is the line that restricts the redrawing to the rectangle *r*, which is produced from the union of the old rectangle and the new rectangle. Any call to **paint( )** coming after this line will be restricted to this rectangle.

5.9 Summary

This chapter has examined the Font class, drawing methods and taken a look at some simple animations. We should know how to bring a graphic file to the screen, how to use graphics primitives to build up complex shapes and patterns. We know how to animate pictures and we have looked at the techniques of animation, including the use of MediaTracker objects to monitor the loading of pictures, the use of Threads to control the speed of an animation, the use of double buffering in conjunction with overriding the **update( )** method to smooth animation and the use of clipping to reduce the workload on the computer.

5.10 Exercises

1. Create an animation using only double buffering and a thread.

2. Create an animation that moves a small picture of a snake across a background picture of a desert.

3. Draw a circle, using the rounded rectangle method.

4. Draw a grid for a game of Os and Xs.

5. Write a method that will draw an X or a O in a particular place on the screen.The method should take x, y coordinates as arguments.

6. Modify the Bouncing Text applet so that the text moves in a diagonal and bounces off the sides as well as the top and bottom of the applet area.

6

THE AWT

6.1 Aims of this chapter

The aim of this chapter is to examine in detail some of the
components of the AWT that we have glanced at in our example
programs. We will be looking at the familiar components that
make up a windows interface, such as Buttons, Checkboxes,
Scrollbars, etc. and looking at the **Container** class and its
subclasses **Panel** and **Window**. We will be looking specifically
at Applet programming using the event model provided in the
JDK 1.0. In the next chapter we will look at the event model
provided by JDK 1.1.

6.2 Welcome to the AWT

We have touched lightly on the Java AWT in previous chapters,
and we know already that it is the AWT that deals with Java's
ability to provide portable interfaces rendered in the style of the
host operating system. The AWT contains classes that fall broadly
into three categories. The first, **Graphics** we have already looked
at. The second category, **Components** contains the GUI
components commonly found in windows systems, such as menus,
buttons, etc. These components are added to a **Container** class

such as **Frame** or **Panel** and arranged using classes from the third category **Layout Managers**, of which we have already used **BorderLayout** and **FlowLayout**.

We are about to meet **GridLayout**, **CardLayout**, **GridBag-Layout** and **GridBagConstraints** for the first time.

——6.3 A Graphical User Interface——

The picture shows the latest stage in development of the Drag Racing game. The user interface that we designed earlier has been integrated with the action area of the game itself.

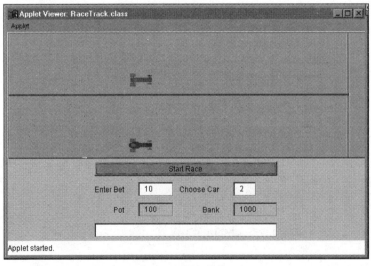

Drag racing GUI

The code for this is shown below – don't panic – although it looks like heavy going, it is actually quite simple. We will look at everything that went into this program on its own, and examine the implications of bundling it all together.

```
import java.applet.Applet;
import java.awt.*;
```

```java
public class RaceTrack extends Applet
{
    RaceTrackCanvas animation;
    private Label betLabel, potLabel, bankLabel, carLabel;
    private TextField betField, carField, potField, bankField,winnerField;
    private Button goButton;
    Panel p;

    public void init( )
    {
        animation = new RaceTrackCanvas( );
        animation.init(this);
        setLayout(new BorderLayout( ));
        p = new Panel( );
        p.setBackground(Color.lightGray);
        GridBagLayout grid = new GridBagLayout();
        p.setLayout(grid);
        betLabel = new Label("Enter Bet");
        carLabel = new Label( "Choose Car");
        potLabel = new Label("Pot");
        bankLabel = new Label("Bank");

        betField = new TextField(5);
        carField = new TextField(2);
        potField = new TextField(5);
        bankField = new TextField(7);
        winnerField = new TextField(20);

        potField.setEditable(false);
        bankField.setEditable(false);

        goButton = new Button("Start Race");

        GridBagConstraints gbc = new GridBagConstraints( );

        gbc.fill = GridBagConstraints.BOTH;
        gbc.insets = new Insets(5, 5, 5, 5);
        add(goButton, grid, gbc, 0, 0, 4, 1);

        gbc.fill = GridBagConstraints.NONE;
        gbc.anchor = GridBagConstraints.EAST;
        add(betLabel, grid, gbc, 0, 1, 1, 1);
```

```
      gbc.anchor = GridBagConstraints.WEST;
      add(betField, grid, gbc, 1, 1, 1, 1);

      gbc.anchor = GridBagConstraints.EAST;
      add(carLabel, grid, gbc, 2, 1, 1, 1);

      gbc.anchor = GridBagConstraints.WEST;
      add(carField, grid, gbc, 3, 1, 1, 1);

      gbc.anchor = GridBagConstraints.EAST;
      add(potLabel, grid, gbc, 0, 2, 1, 1);

      gbc.anchor = GridBagConstraints.WEST;
      add(potField, grid, gbc, 1, 2, 1, 1);

      gbc.anchor = GridBagConstraints.EAST;
      add(bankLabel, grid, gbc,2, 2, 1, 1);

      gbc.anchor = GridBagConstraints.WEST;
      add(bankField, grid, gbc, 3, 2, 1, 1);

      gbc.fill = GridBagConstraints.BOTH;
      add(winnerField, grid, gbc, 0, 3, 4, 1);

      betField.setText("");
      potField.setText("100");
      bankField.setText("1000");

      add("Center", animation);
      add("South", p);
   }
   private void add(Component c, GridBagLayout grid,
         GridBagConstraints gbc, int x, int y, int w, int h)
   {
      gbc.gridx = x;
      gbc.gridy = y;
      gbc.gridwidth = w;
      gbc.gridheight = h;
      grid.setConstraints( c, gbc);
      p.add(c);
   }
}
```

```java
class RaceTrackCanvas extends Canvas
{
   RaceTrack holder;

   Image Track, Car1, Car2;
   int XPos, YPos;

   public void init(RaceTrack app)
   {
      resize(600,270);
      setBackground(Color.darkGray);
      holder = app;
      Track = holder.getImage(app.getCodeBase( ), "Track.gif");
      Car1 = holder.getImage(app.getCodeBase( ), "Redcar.gif");
      Car2 = holder.getImage(app.getCodeBase( ), "Bluecar.gif");
      XPos = 30;
      YPos = 30;
   }

   public void paint(Graphics g)
   {
      Dimension d = size( );
      int w;
      int h;
      w = Track.getWidth(this);
      h = Track.getHeight(this);
      if ((w>0) && (h>0))
      {
         g.drawImage(Track, XPos, YPos, this);
      }

      w = Car1.getWidth(this);
      h = Car2.getHeight(this);

      if ((w>0) && (h>0))
      {
         g.drawImage(Car1, XPos, YPos +25, this);
         g.drawImage(Car2, YPos, YPos +130, this);
      }
   }
} // end class
```

The first thing to notice is that we have defined a new class called **animation**, which extends **Canvas**. This class holds the graphics and will eventually implement **Runnable** and control the race.

Why do we need a canvas?

——— 6.4 Panels and canvases ———

Panels are descended from the **Container** class, which means that we can use a panel as a container for components. Since **Applet** is derived from the class **Panel**, we can use an applet as a container for GUI widgets without declaring any new panel. We can also declare multiple panels and place them upon an applet, positioning them with a **Layout Manager**.

Canvases are descended from **Component**, but not from **Container**. A canvas has its own graphics context and is used to provide a dedicated drawing area for graphics as can be seen in the Drag Racing interface. A canvas may not be used as a **Container** object in the same way as a panel.

The programs below illustrate the use of a panel on its own, a canvas on its own and finally a combination of the two together.

Panel

Because the applet is derived from the class **Panel**, we can use it to contain a second panel, which we use to contain a **Label** object. Note that the position of the panels is set by the default Layout Manager provided by **Applet** – **FlowLayout**.

```
import java.awt.*;
import java.applet.Applet;

public class MyPanel extends Applet
{
    Panel p;
    Label text;
```

```
public void init( )
{
  // set colour of Applet background
  setBackground(Color.black);
  // instantiate Panel object
  p = new Panel( );
  // set colour of Panel
  p.setBackground(Color.white);
  // add Panel to Applet
  add(p);
  // instantiate a Label object to be contained by Panel
  text = new Label("This text is contained in a white panel
        contained in a black applet");
  // add Label object to Panel
  p.add(text);
  }
}
```

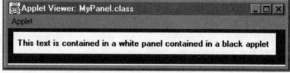

Using a panel in an applet

Canvas

We can create a canvas and set its background colour in the same way that we used in the previous section to create a panel. However, if we want to draw a picture on it, using **paint( )**, as we have in previous examples, we must extend the **Canvas** class and use this extended class in our applet.

Using a canvas to hold graphics

```java
import java.awt.*;
import java.applet.Applet;

public class UsesCanvas extends Applet
{
    // Declare an instance of our extended Canvas class
    DrawCanvas c;

    public void init( )
    {
        setBackground(Color.black);
        // instantiate our extended Canvas class
        c = new DrawCanvas( );
        // initialise Canvas class i.e. Load Picture and set Background
        c.init(this);
        add(c);          // add the Canvas to our Applet
    }
}

class DrawCanvas extends Canvas
{
    Image Peace;

    // Uses methods known only to the containing Applet
    public void init(UsesCanvas app)
    {
        resize( 200, 200);          // sets size of Canvas
        setBackground(Color.white);
        // getImage( ) is an Applet method, not a Canvas method
        Peace = app.getImage(app.getCodeBase( ), "Peace.gif");
    }

    public void paint(Graphics g)
    {
        // Draws on the Canvas
        g.drawImage(Peace, 50, 50, this);
    }
}
```

Nesting components

It is possible to generate sophisticated layouts, by nesting components within one another. In this example, we show a panel and a canvas placed next to one another on an applet.

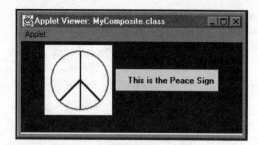

*Nesting components:
canvas and panel on
an applet*

As the applet is itself a panel, the code required to do this is not complex, we use a Layout Manager (**FlowLayout**) to determine where the components should be placed. The only code that has been altered is in the applet's **init( )** method.

```
public class MyComposite extends Applet
{
    DrawCanvas c;
    Panel p;
    Label caption;

    public void init( )
    {
        setLayout(new FlowLayout( ));
        setBackground(Color.black);
        p = new Panel( );
        p.setBackground(Color.yellow);
        caption = new Label("This is the Peace Sign");
        p.add(caption);
        c = new DrawCanvas( );
        c.init(this);
        add(c);
        add(p);
    }
}
```

Suppose we wanted to add a caption at the top of the screen, and preserve the layout of the panel in the illustration at the bottom of the screen? One solution would be to divide the screen into two panels, the first containing the caption and the second containing the other two components.

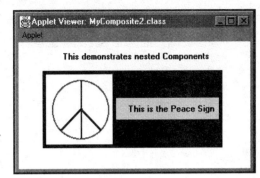

*Nesting components:
canvas and panel on
a panel on an applet*

This is the hierarchy of components now placed on the applet.

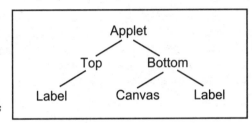

Hierarchy of components

Here is the adjusted **init( )** method.

```
public void init( )
{
    setLayout(new FlowLayout( ));

    Top = new Panel( );
    PageCaption = new Label("This demonstrates nested
    Components");
    Top.add(PageCaption);

    Bottom = new Panel( );
    // set layout and colour of Bottom panel
    Bottom.setLayout(new FlowLayout( ));
    Bottom.setBackground(Color.black);
        p = new Panel( );
        p.setBackground(Color.yellow);
        caption = new Label("This is the Peace Sign");
        p.add(caption);
```

```
    c = new DrawCanvas( );
    c.init(this);
// add components to Bottom Panel
Bottom.add(c);
Bottom.add(p);
// add components to Applet
add(Top);
add(Bottom);
}
```

——— 6.5 Providing interactivity ———

The real power of GUIs lies in the fact that they offer the user an element of control which is not so complicated that they have to divert their attention from the task that is being done to the task of manipulating a computer to do it. This is mainly achieved through choice and selection.

We have seen in the last few examples, how Labels can be used to provide textual information. These may be instructions associated with another component or simply a label for a component. Labels we have used so far have all contained text of some kind and we have seen the method **getText()** demonstrated in Chapter 4 (page 66). We will now take a look at some of the other familiar Windows elements such as Buttons – push buttons, Checkboxes, Choice buttons; using Checkboxes in groups to form radio buttons; and finally scrollable lists.

Push buttons

```
import java.awt.*;
import java.applet.Applet;

public class myButton extends Applet
{
    Button b;
    TextField t;
    int num, result;
```

```
public void init( )
{
   b = new Button("Double");
   t = new TextField(7);
   t.setText("100");
   add(b);
   add(t);
}
public boolean action(Event e, Object o)
{
   if (e.target == b)
   {
   num = Integer.parseInt(t.getText());
   result = num * 2;
   t.setText(Integer.toString(result));
   }
   return true;
}
}
```

This code provides a **TextField** which holds a number. When the 'Double' button, *b*, is pressed, the number is multiplied by two and the new answer displayed. If a further button is needed, *Button b1*, then a further condition would be required in the **action( )** method, beginning:

```
if (e.target == b1)
{
   // Then this sequence of events occur
}
```

You might try rewriting this program adding two more buttons, one to triple the figure and one to return the figure to 0.

Checkboxes

A Checkbox

```java
import java.io.*;
import java.awt.*;
import java.applet.Applet;

public class MyCheckBox extends Applet
{
    Checkbox Bold, Italic;
    TextField t;
    Font f;

    public void init( )
    {
        f = new Font("TimesRoman", Font.PLAIN, 16);
        Bold = new Checkbox("Bold");
        Italic = new Checkbox("Italic");
        t = new TextField(30);

        t.setFont(f);
        t.setText("We're off to see the Wizard!");

        add(t);
        add(Bold);
        add(Italic);
    }

    public boolean action(Event e, Object o)
    {
        int bold, italic;

        if (e.target instanceof Checkbox)
        {
            if ((e.target == Italic) || (e.target == Bold))
            {
            int x = (Bold.getState() ? Font.BOLD : 0)
                + (Italic.getState() ? Font.ITALIC : 0);
            t.setFont(new Font("TimesRoman", x, 16));
            System.out.println("Font Style =" + x);
            }
        }
        return true;
    }
}
```

The only bit of this code that requires explanation should be the **action( )** method. The same result could have been achieved with a series of **if** statements, each one setting the Font explicitly. This would have been repetitive and programmers like to avoid needless repetition. Now, **Font.BOLD**, **Font.PLAIN** and **Font.ITALIC** are actually integer values. This means that we can test for the box being checked and represent the result as a number. For *Bold*, the statement

```
int x = (Bold.getState() ? Font.BOLD : 0)
```

means that if *Bold* is checked, x is equal to 1 (**Font.BOLD**), if it is not checked then x is equal to 0 (**Font.PLAIN**). **Font.ITALIC** = 2 and the combination of both is equal to 3. This construction is very useful when checking a condition with only two outcomes.

The Fonts supported in Java are **TimesRoman** (Times New Roman in Windows systems), **Helvetica** (Arial in Windows), and **Courier**. For reasons to do with internationalisation, these Font names are to be replaced by **serif**, **sansserif** and **monospaced**, which are generic types easily mappable onto any alphabet.

The Font Style example is adequate for its purpose, but what if we wanted to change the font itself, or the size? Obviously we cannot have a font that is both Helvetica and Times New Roman in the way that we can have a font that is both bold and italic. There are two alternatives, either we write some extra code to set the other options to false or we look to the Java libraries again. We have two ready made constructs for this eventuality. The first is known as a Choice Button.

Choice buttons

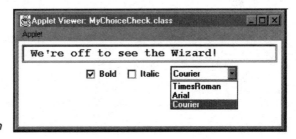

A Choice button

```java
import java.awt.*;
import java.applet.Applet;

public class MyChoiceCheck extends Applet
{
   Choice FontName;
   Checkbox Bold, Italic;
   TextField t;
   String font;
   int x;

   public void init( )
   {
      FontName = new Choice( );
      FontName.addItem("TimesRoman");
      FontName.addItem("Helvetica");
      FontName.addItem("Courier");

      Bold = new Checkbox("Bold");
      Italic = new Checkbox("Italic");

      t = new TextField(40);
      t.setFont(new Font("TimesRoman", Font.PLAIN, 16));
      t.setText("We're off to see the Wizard!");

      add(t);
      add(Bold);
      add(Italic);
      add(FontName);
   }

   public boolean action(Event e, Object o)
   {
      int bold, italic;

      if (e.target instanceof Checkbox)
      {
         if ((e.target == Italic) || (e.target == Bold))
         {
         x = (Bold.getState() ? Font.BOLD : 0)
            + (Italic.getState() ? Font.ITALIC : 0);
         }
      }
```

```
    if (e.target instanceof Choice)
       font=(FontName.getSelectedItem( ));
    t.setFont(new Font(font, x, 16));
    true;
  }
 }
```

Adding the Choice box is relatively straightforward, we declare a new **Choice** object and itemise the choices individually, adding them explicitly to the object. When we get to the action method, things become a little more complex. In our previous program, we were able to use local variables to control the font style. All variables were declared inside the **action( )** method, because they were not needed anywhere else.

In this example we have to combine the settings from the check boxes with the settings from the **Choice** object. Because **action()** is called every time the Checkbox is checked or the Choicebox chosen, we need to save the state of the previous settings, otherwise when we choose a new Typeface, the text will revert to plain even though Bold might be checked in the applet.

The simple way to get around this problem is to make the settings global, i.e. declare them at the beginning of the program.

Radio buttons

Radio buttons are used when there are a limited number of mutually exclusive choices, for example on a mail order form, the credit card is likely to be Visa, MasterCard or Access, but never more than one at a time.

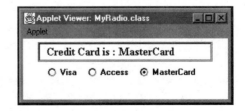

A Radio button

```java
import java.awt.*;
import java.applet.Applet;

public class MyRadio extends Applet
{
    CheckboxGroup radio;
    Checkbox Visa, Access, MasterCard;
    TextField t;
    Font f;

    public void init( )
    {
        f = new Font("TimesRoman", Font.BOLD, 16);
        t = new TextField(30);
        t.setFont(f);
        t.setText("Credit Card is ");

        radio = new CheckboxGroup( );

        add(t);
        add(Visa = new Checkbox("Visa", radio, false));
        add(Access = new Checkbox("Access", radio, false));
        add(MasterCard = new Checkbox("MasterCard", radio, false));
    }
    public boolean action(Event e, Object o)
    {
        if ( e.target instanceof Checkbox)
        {
            if (Visa.getState( ) == true)
                t.setText("Credit Card is : Visa");
            if (Access.getState( ) == true)
                t.setText("Credit Card is : Access");
            if (MasterCard.getState( ) == true)
                t.setText("Credit Card is : MasterCard");
        }
        return true;
    }
}
```

A set of Radio buttons is actually a group of Checkboxes, treated
in exactly the same way except that we register them with a
CheckboxGroup( ) object when we add them to the applet:

```java
add(MasterCard = new Checkbox("MasterCard", radio, false));
```

The arguments taken by Checkbox here are the label attached
to it, the group it belongs to and a boolean describing whether or
not it is checked. We have previously declared radio as being a
CheckboxGroup( ) with the line:

```
radio = new CheckboxGroup( );
```

Lists

We are now going to have a look at lists, the context we are
going to look at them in is that of a 'shopping basket' style
application. This one will allow us to choose the ingredients for
a breakfast from one list, and see them displayed in another.

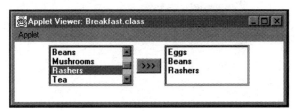

A list

```
import java.io.*;
import java.awt.*;
import java.applet.Applet;

public class Breakfast extends Applet
{
    List ingredients, meal;
    Button Move;

    public void init( )
    {
        ingredients = new List(4, false);
        meal = new List(4, false);

        Move = new Button(">>>");

        ingredients.addItem("Corn Flakes");
        ingredients.addItem("Muesli");
        ingredients.addItem("Eggs");
        ingredients.addItem("Beans");
```

```
    ingredients.addItem("Mushrooms");
    ingredients.addItem("Rashers");
    ingredients.addItem("Tea");
    ingredients.addItem("Coffee");
    ingredients.addItem("Toast");
    ingredients.addItem("Croissant");

    add(ingredients);
    add(Move);
    add(meal);
}
public boolean action(Event e, Object o)
{
    if (e.target instanceof List)
{
    if (o.equals("Beans"))
    {
       meal.addItem("Beans");
    }
}

    if (e.target == Move)
    {
       meal.addItem(ingredients.getSelectedItem( ));
    }
    return true;
}
}
```

This example sets up a list with the line:

```
ingredients = new List(4, false);
```

The arguments given to **List( )** represent the number of items
visible, and a boolean variable indicating whether multiple
selection is allowed. Items are added to the list as Strings.

The **action( )** method illustrates two ways of dealing with events,
the first way checks for double click on an item in the list – 'Beans'
and acts on it (Each item is an object in its own right which is
passed to the **action( )** method.) Notice that we are comparing
an object to a string – this requires us to use the **equals( )** method
rather than the == operator. If we were to use the == operator, it

would return true only if both references refer to the same object in memory. There is a difference between comparing two values and two references to a value. For this reason, when testing a list item or button label for equality, always use the **equals( )** method.

The second way is more user friendly in that people are used to using buttons to move items from box to box in software. The second method also allows us to act on multiple selections – if we have set the boolean to *true* in the declaration. For multiple selections, the **List** method **getSelectedItem( )**, which returns a *single* String, is replaced by **getSelectedItems( )**, which returns an *array* of type String.

—————— 6.6 Summary ——————

This chapter has covered the components section of the Java Abstract Windowing Toolkit. We have looked at the **Container** class **Panel** and demonstrated that an applet is a panel and that a panel can contain other components, including other panels. A Canvas has been shown to be a useful component for displaying graphic files. We have looked in detail at the Font class and demonstrated the preferred use of generic types instead of platform specific font names.

GUIs, or graphical user interfaces, are made up of components. We have looked at the basic components provided by the AWT, including buttons, checkboxes, choice buttons, labels, lists and in previous chapters, the text Components, textField and textArea. We began the chapter with a look at a user interface for a game that demonstrated the use of a canvas and a panel, controlled by two layout managers, one to control the positioning of the two major components, panel and canvas, and another, **gridBagLayout** to control the layout of the buttons and textFields on the control panel. The next chapter will examine Layout Managers in detail.

──────── 6.7 Exercises ────────

1. Add a List containing Font Size to the example on page 121, and make it change the size of the font in the message displayed. To maintain good practice, you should make the TimesRoman menu item call the *serif* font, Helvetica the *sansserif* and courier the *monospaced*.

2. In the Breakfast example, work out a method of displaying the price of each item in the list. Have the computer display the total price of a breakfast.

3. Create an interface with three buttons on three panels, the button on each panel should change the background colour of the panel.

4. In the breakfast example, allow multiple selection and implement a method to add the items selected to the second list. (Clue: you need an array to hold the items.)

5. Write a program that will work out the repayments on a mortgage over 10 years, 25 years and 35 years – presume simple interest! The program should allow the user to input the total amount borrowed and the interest rate. The length of the loan should be made via a radio button or a choice box.

7

LAYOUT MANAGERS

7.1 Aims of this chapter

We have looked at the components and containers used to build GUIs, and we have seen an example of a GUI 'in action', utilising layout managers to control the position of the various elements on the screen. We will now take a closer look at the Layout Managers provided by the Java AWT. These are:

FlowLayout: Default manager, arranges elements left to right and top to bottom where there is more than one row.

BorderLayout: Arranges elements into five areas, North, South, East, West and Center. Center expands to fill unallocated space.

GridLayout: Elements are arranged in equal rows and columns the number of which is defined by the programmer.

CardLayout: Elements are arranged into a 'stack' where only the top card is visible. Usually used to stack containers so that a part of a screen can be changed.

GridBagLayout: The 'Mother of all Layout Managers', this is the most flexible and inevitably the most complicated. Allows the programmer to define a grid based on the smallest component and to specify how many cells each component will fill in a horizontal and vertical direction. Attempting to use this manager without a sketch of the proposed interface will seriously damage your mental well-being!

7.2 FlowLayout

The pictured applet demonstrates the use of FlowLayout. Three panels, in different colours have been placed upon the applet. The applet's Layout Manager has been set to align all elements to the left in the code:

```
setLayout(new FlowLayout(FlowLayout.LEFT));
```

The alignment property must be in capital letters. FlowLayout defaults to CENTER alignment. If we had wanted our elements to be centred, we could have left this line out altogether, as FlowLayout is applets' default Layout Manager.

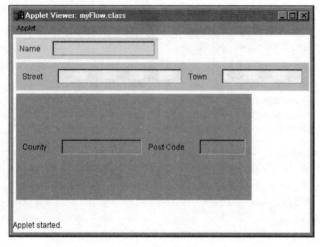

Three panels arranged with FlowLayout

The second panel illustrates that we can control the horizontal and vertical spacing of elements contained in the Panel:

```
p1.setLayout(new FlowLayout(FlowLayout.CENTER, 10, 10));
```

The last argument specifies the vertical spacing, the second argument the horizontal. The third panel illustrates the effect of increasing the vertical spacing.

```java
import java.awt.*;
import java.applet.Applet;

public class myFlow extends Applet
{
    // declare all elements
    private TextField name, street, town, county, postCode;
    private Label nameLabel, streetLabel, townLabel, countyLabel;
    private Label postCodeLabel;
    private Panel p, p1, p2;

    public void init( )
    {
        // set Layout alignment  for the whole applet
        setLayout(new FlowLayout(FlowLayout.LEFT));

        // instantiate first panel and set background colour
        p = new Panel( );
        p.setBackground(Color.yellow);

        // instantiate second panel, set colour and specify spacing
        p1 = new Panel( );
        p1.setBackground(Color.pink);
        p1.setLayout(new FlowLayout(FlowLayout.CENTER, 10, 10));

        p2 = new Panel( );
        p2.setBackground(Color.green);
        p2.setLayout(new FlowLayout(FlowLayout.RIGHT, 10, 70));

        // instantiate all elements
        name = new TextField(20);
        name.setEditable(true);
        street = new TextField(25);
        street.setEditable(true);
        town = new TextField(15);
        town.setEditable(true);
        county = new TextField(15);
        county.setEditable(true);
        postCode = new TextField(7);
        postCode.setEditable(true);

        nameLabel = new Label("Name");
        streetLabel = new Label("Street");
        townLabel = new Label("Town");
```

```
        countyLabel = new Label("County");
        postCodeLabel = new Label("Post Code");

        // add elements to their panels
        p.add(nameLabel);
        p.add(name);
        p1.add(streetLabel);
        p1.add(street);
        p1.add(townLabel);
        p1.add(town);

        p2.add(countyLabel);
        p2.add(county);
        p2.add(postCodeLabel);
        p2.add(postCode);

        // add completed panels to the applet
        add(p);
        add(p1);
        add(p2);
    }
}
```

───────── 7.3 BorderLayout ─────────

BorderLayout is the default layout manager for Windows and the Window subclass **Frame**, which are mainly used in applications. Applets do not tend to use Window and Frames because applets are embedded in the context of an HTML page, whereas applications require window management (a Frame can be used with an applet to create a free floating 'window' associated with the applet). BorderLayout may still be used as a layout manager for Applets, where circumstances require it.

The example shows a typical BorderLayout. There are up to five areas in a BorderLayout. When all five are used, the arrangement will look like the pictured applet. If the East or West areas are missing, the Center expands to take up the slack. If North or South are missing, the Center and East/West fill the remaining space.

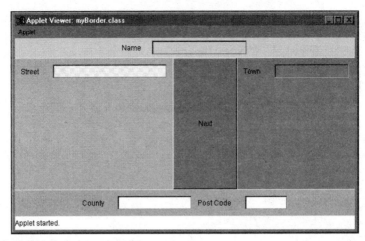

The BorderLayout

The code for this applet is not substantially different. The fields have been distributed among four panels and a button has been introduced for the **Center** position. The look of a Border Layout depends on the dimensions of the applet area or its window. The **Center** position is the last to be calculated and its size depends on how much room is left after the other elements have been arranged.

```
setLayout(new BorderLayout(1, 1));
```

is used instead of

```
setLayout(new FlowLayout(FlowLayout.LEFT);
```

The arguments given to BorderLayout control the width and height of the border separating each component from the nest. In this case one pixel has been chosen.

The allocation of elements to areas is done when they are added to the applet:

```
add("North", p);
add("West", p1);
add("East", p2);
add("South", p3);
add("Center", b);
```

where *b* in the last line is the button.

This layout manager comes into its own when the layout includes components such as scroll bars, as each area is calculated according to the size of the element it contains.

7.4 GridLayout

GridLayout, predictably arranges the components in a programmer specified grid. Each component is the same size and we can specify horizontal and vertical spacing between components. This layout is ideal for creating displays of buttons or keypads as seen in the calculator applet. Illustrated is a part of a computer keyboard.

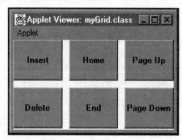

Buttons arranged with GridLayout

```java
import java.awt.*;
import java.applet.Applet;

public class myGrid extends Applet
{
    // declare variables
    private Button  b1, b2, b3, b4, b5, b6;

    public void init( )
    {
        // instantiate Buttons
        b1 = new Button("Insert");
        b2 = new Button("Home");
        b3 = new Button("Page Up");
        b4 = new Button("Delete");
        b5 = new Button("End");
        b6 = new Button("Page Down");
```

```
/* Set layout to 2 rows and 3 columns, separated by 10
    pixels each way. */
setLayout( new GridLayout(2, 3, 10, 10));

// add buttons to applet
add(b1);
add(b2);
add(b3);
add(b4);
add(b5);
add(b6);
   }
 }
```

————————7.5 CardLayout————————

The CardLayout manager works by storing the components in a stack, like a pack of cards, so that only the top component is visible. It offers a convenient way to let the user navigate through a series of screens from a list, or via push buttons. An example of such an application would be a personal information manager where the user selects Diary, Calendar or Notepad and the appropriate format is summoned to the screen.

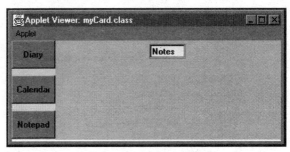

A PIM using CardLayout

In the pictured applet, clicking on one of the buttons to the left, will bring the appropriate card to the top of the pile. At the moment the Notepad is displayed.

```java
import java.awt.*;
import java.applet.Applet;

public class myCard extends Applet
{
    // declare all the variables for the program
    private TextField DText, CText, NText;
    private TextArea DEntry;
    private Button  Diary, Cal, Note;
    private Panel Bpanel, Cards, Dpanel, Cpanel, Npanel;
    private CardLayout c;

    public void init( )
    {
        /* We'll use a border layout to position the control panel
           and the 'pack' of cards */
        setLayout(new BorderLayout());

        // set up the control panel, use a grid layout for the buttons
        Diary = new Button("Diary");
        Cal = new Button("Calendar");
        Note = new Button("Notepad");

        Bpanel = new Panel( );
        Bpanel.setBackground(Color.yellow);
        Bpanel.setLayout( new GridLayout( 3, 1, 10, 10));
        Bpanel.add(Diary);
        Bpanel.add(Cal);
        Bpanel.add(Note);

        // now set up the components contained by each card.

        // Diary Card
        Dpanel = new Panel( );
        DEntry = new TextArea(5,20);
        DText = new TextField("April 1");
        Dpanel.add(DText);
        Dpanel.add(DEntry);

        // Calendar Card
        Cpanel = new Panel( );
        CText = new TextField("1997");
        Cpanel.setBackground(Color.green);
        Cpanel.add(CText);
```

```
// Notepad Card
Npanel = new Panel( );
NText = new TextField("Notes");
Npanel.setBackground(Color.pink);
Npanel.add(NText);

// Now create a container to hold the cards
Cards = new Panel( );

// instantiate a layout manager for it
c = new CardLayout( );
Cards.setLayout(c);

// now add the predefined cards
Cards.add("Diary", Dpanel);
Cards.add("Calendar", Cpanel);
Cards.add("Notes", Npanel);

 // finally, add the control panel and the pack of cards
add("West", Bpanel);
add("Center", Cards);
}

// show the card manager what to do when the button is pressed!
public boolean action( Event e, Object o)
{
   if (e.target == Diary)
   {
      c.show(Cards, "Diary");
   }
   else if (e.target == Cal)
   {
      c.show(Cards, "Calendar");
   }
      else if (e.target == Note)
   {
      c.show(Cards, "Notes");
   }
   return true;
   }
 }
```

Probably the best way of coding a CardLayout is to code the hierarchy of components separately – deal with the top level panels first and then add the individual cards, rather than attempting to code the whole thing in one go. The hierarchy of components in the example program is this:

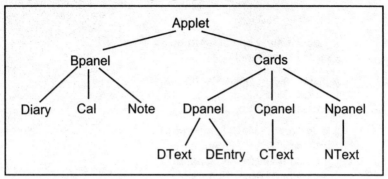

Component hierarchy for CardLayout

This applet is only a skeleton, if it were to be developed properly, the hierarchy would extend several layers deeper, as components were added to give it the required functionality. It is therefore essential to work out what elements are included at which level before sitting down to code it. One useful strategy is to insert the panels you require before any other components. By setting the background colours temporarily, you can quickly see that your code is working properly, before you begin to add the detail.

The most noteworthy part of the code is the event handling, because the layout manager is working in response to events, we must be able to pass messages back to it – in this case the message is:

```
c.show(Cards, "Calendar");
```

where the button clicked is 'Cal'. The Layout Manager has previously been assigned to a variable *c*. Methods available to CardLayout include **show(Container,name)**, **next(Container)** and **previous(Container)**. The Container is the component that contains the panels, the name is only used with the **show( )** method, and is allocated to the component when it is added to its container. The components of a CardLayout are recorded by the Layout Manager in the order that they are added.

```
Cards.add("Calendar", Cpanel);
```

where *Cards* is the container panel, *Cpanel* is the panel being added and 'Calendar' is the name by which we will refer to it in the **show( )** method.

7.6 GridBagLayout

GridBagLayout is the most flexible of Layout Managers, but also the most complex. It builds on the GridLayout in that the layout is based on a grid, but differs in that components can fill more than one cell in the grid and therefore vary in size in the display. The way to devise a GridBagLayout is to draw the interface on paper first, and then make a grid that if possible encloses the smallest component. If that is not possible, then it should be based on either the width or the height of the smallest component.

Design grid for GridBagLayout

In this grid, the Start Race button begins at column 0 and ends in column 3. Like arrays, the first element is 0, not 1.

Having decided on an appropriate grid, we instantiate a **GridBagLayout** object. We do not tell it how many rows and columns it is dealing with yet, that is the job of a separate **GridBagConstraints** object.

```
GridBagLayout grid = new GridBagLayout( );
```

We now have a layout manager called *grid* and we assign it to the panel it will be managing, in this case, *p*.

```
p.setLayout(grid);
```

The next step is to construct a **GridBagConstraints** object. This will pass all the parameters for each cell in the grid, to the **GridBagLayout** manager.

GridBagConstraints

```
GridBagConstraints gbc = new GridBagConstraints( );
```

constructs the object. Now for every element in the display, we have to pass the following information:

gridx	starting column
gridy	starting row
gridwidth	number of columns spanned
gridheight	number of rows spanned
weightx	amount of horizontal space allowed for expansion as a priority
weighty	amount of vertical space allowed for expansion as a priority

In addition to this, we can also pass:

ipadx	internal horizontal padding
ipady	internal vertical padding
insets	margins to appear on all sides of component
anchor	positions component in larger cell, using compass points and centre as in GridLayout
fill	specifies direction in which a component is allowed to grow if space is available. This could be NONE, BOTH, HORIZONTAL or VERTICAL.

Clearly there is much room for confusion here, as well as the potential for reams of repetitive code. The best way to approach it is to override the **add( )** function so that we can pass the component name, its position, breadth and depth at least as parameters. These are the vital parameters – everything else can be seen as 'fine tuning'. The idea is to get a layout that is close to ideal and then specify some of these other variables.

By doing this, we can convert:

```
gbc.gridx = 0;
gbc.gridy = 0;
gbc.gridwidth = 4;
gbc.gridheight = 1;
Button goButton = new Button("Start");
grid.setConstraints( b, gbc);
p.add(goButton);
```

which we would have to repeat for every component, into:

```
add(goButton, grid, gbc, 0, 0, 4, 1);
```

The redefined **add( )** function looks like this:

```
private void add(Component c, GridBagLayout grid,
GridBagConstraints gbc, int x, int y, int w, int h)
{
   gbc.gridx = x;
   gbc.gridy = y;
   gbc.gridwidth = w;
   gbc.gridheight = h;
   grid.setConstraints(c, gbc);
   p.add(c);
}
```

This add function allows us quickly to add all the components in a style of code which we can easily follow.

```
add(goButton, grid, gbc, 0, 0, 4, 1);
add(betLabel, grid, gbc, 0, 1, 1, 1);
add(betField, grid, gbc, 1, 1, 1, 1);
add(carLabel, grid, gbc, 2, 1, 1, 1);
add(carField, grid, gbc, 3, 1, 1, 1);
add(potLabel, grid, gbc, 0, 2, 1, 1);
add(potField, grid, gbc, 1, 2, 1, 1);
add(bankLabel, grid, gbc,2, 2, 1, 1);
add(bankField, grid, gbc, 3, 2, 1, 1);
add(winnerField, grid, gbc, 0, 3, 4, 1);
```

Once this is in place, we should have a working program. To fine tune it, we can add the details immediately before the component we want to alter.

```
gbc.fill = GridBagConstraints.BOTH;
gbc.insets = new Insets(5, 5, 5, 5);
add(goButton, grid, gbc, 0, 0, 4, 1);
add(betLabel, grid, gbc, 0, 1, 1, 1);
      ... etc, etc.
```

sets the **fill** and **insets** variables for all components until a newer instruction is placed.

```
gbc.fill = GridBagConstraints.BOTH;
```

```
gbc.insets = new Insets(5, 5, 5, 5);
add(goButton, grid, gbc, 0, 0, 4, 1);
gbc.insets = new Insets(10,10,10,10);
add(betLabel, grid, gbc, 0, 1, 1, 1);
```

the effect of the italicised line above is to alter the **insets** value from 5 all round, to 10 all round.

```
gbc.anchor = GridBagConstraints.WEST;
```

inserting this line before an **add()** will display the following components to the left of the cell.

The example at the beginning of Chapter 6 contains the full code for the Drag Racing interface, using a variety of layout managers to place components correctly.

——————— 7.7 Summary ———————

We have now dealt with all the layout managers in some detail. The essential lesson is always opt for the simplest layout manager. The second most important thing is always put some time into thinking about the design of your interface – you will quickly tie yourself in knots by attempting to code interfaces from scratch. It doesn't matter if you are not the greatest draughtsman in the world, anyone can benefit from rough sketches that show proportionate size and position of elements.

——————— 7.8 Exercises ———————

1. Design an interface for an on-line art gallery. You will need to see the picture and read some details about the artist.

2. Design an interface for an on-line catalogue. Half the screen should contain the items for sale, the other half should contain fields allowing the user to fill in their name, address and credit card details and buttons to select different pages from the catalogue.

3. Design an interface for a car dashboard. It should contain the speedometer and rev counter as large central objects, surrounded by fuel level, oil warning, brake light, head light, indicator and temperature gauges.

4. Design the layout for an E-mail applet. There should be space for the user to write the message, and TextFields for the user to fill in the E-mail address, the Description and the Copy to address. There should be buttons to send the message and to clear the screen.

5. Design an interface for a travel agent that allows the user to select items from a series of lists and buttons. The lists should be flight details, destination, length of stay, self-catering or half board, and dates of stay.

8

GUI DESIGN AND EVENT HANDLING

8.1 Aims of this chapter

Central to the focus of this chapter is the new event handling model released with JDK 1.1. We have concentrated on applet programming where the deprecated methods are still current, but it is expected that the new model will eventually replace the methods we have used so far.

In this chapter we will be looking at certain applications in order to demonstrate the new event model in an environment where it can be guaranteed to work, as well as applets. The first part of the chapter will concentrate on the JDK 1.0 event model in order to look at one way that GUI events can be trapped and dealt with. The JDK 1.1 offers several improvements, which may appear more sensible in comparison.

We will look at the use of Frames in applications and some of the advanced widgets available in the AWT, including Menus, scrollbars and dialog boxes. Following this we will examine the JDK 1.0 event model as it is used to detect keyboard events and mouse events and finally examine the differences in the new event model and rewrite some of our examples as 1.1 compliant programs.

8.2 Frames

A **Frame** in Java is a subclass of **Window**, and is used either as a basis for a Windows-style application, or to provide an applet with a free floating extra window.

First we return to basics for a look at a simple application. The important thing about frame-based applications is that we must provide a means to close them. This is done in JDK 1.0 through an event handler, **handleEvent(Event e)** which ends with the line:

```
return super.handleEvent(e);
```

this passes unhandled events, i.e. those that do not close the window, back to the superclass where they are allocated to the appropriate event handler.

```
import java.awt.*;

class myFrame extends Frame
{
   public static void main(String[ ] args)
   {
      Frame f = new myFrame( );
      f.setBackground(Color.yellow);
      f.pack( );
      f.show( );
   }
   public void paint(Graphics g)
   {
      g.drawString("This is a simple frame", 35, 90);
   }
   public boolean handleEvent(Event e)
   {
      if (e.id == Event.WINDOW_DESTROY)
         System.exit(0);
      return super.handleEvent(e);
   }
}
```

The next example uses the same frame, this time invoked from an applet. There are some important differences in the class **myFrame**. Firstly the **main** method has gone. It is replaced by a constructor method which is called in the applet's **action( )** method, when the frame is called. Secondly, in the frame's **handleEvent( )** method, we have replaced:

```
System.exit(0);
```

with

```
hide( );
dispose( );
```

The reason for this is that we only want to close the window, not the entire applet. The call to **System** would dispose of all resources associated with the window, including the program that called it. We would prefer the applet to continue running until we have finished using it!

```java
import java.awt.*;
import java.applet.Applet;

public class myAppletFrame extends Applet
{
    private myFrame f;
    private Button b;

    public void init( )
    {
        b = new Button("Click me");
        add(b);
    }
    public boolean action(Event e, Object o)
    {
        if (e.target == b)
            f = new myFrame( );
        return true;
    }
}

class myFrame extends Frame
{
    public myFrame( )
    {
        setBackground(Color.yellow);
        pack( );
        show( );
    }
```

```java
public void paint(Graphics g)
{
    g.drawString("This is a simple frame", 35, 90);
}
public boolean handleEvent(Event e)
{
    if (e.id == Event.WINDOW_DESTROY)
    {
        hide( );
        dispose( );
    }
    return super.handleEvent(e);
}
}
```

8.3 Menus

Menus are probably the most ubiquitous feature of GUI programs, yet in Java can only be used with Frames. This effectively restricts the use of menus to applications.

A Menu is itself made up of components – at top level **MenuComponent** is extended to provide **MenuItem** and **MenuBar**. **MenuItem** is extended to provide **Menu** and **CheckboxMenuItem** (items that toggle between two states).

In the picture we have a MenuBar which supports three Menus, Breakfast, Lunch and Action. The Breakfast Menu has been accessed, showing a number of MenuItems and three CheckboxMenu Items.

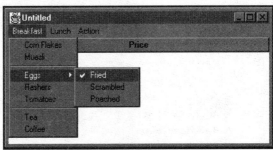

A Menu

The coding is very simple. Declare the MenuBar, then one at a time add the Menus and their MenuItems. It is not syntactically necessary to code in this order, but by nesting the sub-menus, you can see at a glance that all the intended items are in the correct menus. When the MenuItems have been added, the Menu is added to the MenuBar. The final task is to write event handling code for all choices.

Here is the complete code, again using the JDK 1.0 Event model.

```
import java.awt.*;
import java.io.*;

public class myMenu extends Frame
{
    double price = 0.00;
    Button b;

    public myMenu( )
    {
        // Declare MenuBar object
        MenuBar mb = new MenuBar( );

        // Declare Menu object
        Menu B = new Menu("Breakfast");

        // Add items to Menu object
        B.add(new MenuItem("Corn Flakes"));
        B.add(new MenuItem("Muesli"));
        B.addSeparator( );

        // This will be a submenu, indented for ease of reading
            Menu e = new Menu("Eggs");
            e.add(new CheckboxMenuItem("Fried"));
            e.add(new CheckboxMenuItem("Scrambled"));
            e.add(new CheckboxMenuItem("Poached"));

        // Add submenu defined above, to Menu object
        B.add(e);

        // Add more items
        B.add(new MenuItem("Rashers"));
        B.add(new MenuItem("Tomatoes"));
        B.addSeparator();
        B.add(new MenuItem("Tea"));
```

```
B.add(new MenuItem("Coffee"));

// add Breakfast Menu to Menu Bar
mb.add(B);

// Create and add Lunch menu
Menu L = new Menu("Lunch");
L.add(new MenuItem("Steak"));
L.add(new MenuItem("Pasta"));
mb.add(L);

// Create and add Action Menu
Menu A = new Menu("Action");
A.add(new MenuItem("Bill"));
mb.add(A);

// use Frame method to construct object
setMenuBar(mb);

b = new Button("Cancel");
add("North", b);
}
/* As an example, we'll attach a price to one item only, and
   use the action method as a quick Bill calculator */
public boolean action(Event e, Object o)
{
   if (e.target instanceof Button)
   {
      if( e.target == b)
      {
         price = 0.0;
         System.out.println("Your tray is empty - You may
            start choosing again");
      }
   }
   else if (e.target instanceof MenuItem)
   {
   if( o.equals("Rashers"))
      {
         // price = price + 2.25
         price += 2.25;
      }
```

```
    if( o.equals("Bill"))
      {
         System.out.println("Price is: " + price);
      }
    }
    return true;
}
public boolean handleEvent(Event e)
{
    if (e.id == Event.WINDOW_DESTROY)
    {
    System.exit(0);
    return true;
    }
    return super.handleEvent(e);
}
public static void main(String[ ] args)
{
    Frame f = new myMenu( );
    f.pack( );
    f.show( );
  }
}
```

────────── 8.4 Scrollbars ──────────

Scrollbars can be used for two distinct purposes, either to move
the contents of a window in a vertical or horizontal direction, or
as a slider control. This duality is available because the scrollbar
getValue( ) method returns an integer value. Moving a large
canvas within a small window is basically a matter of adding
the integer values provided by horizontal and vertical scrollbars
onto the x,y coordinates of the canvas contents.

To illustrate the use of a scrollbar as a slider control, we could
rewrite the temperature conversion program so that the
Centigrade value is input via a scrollbar.

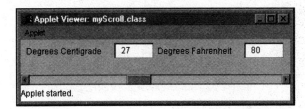

Temperature converter with slider control

A basic layout manager has been used to make the applet look presentable, but the changes to the actual temperature converter are quite straightforward.

A Scrollbar is declared, and deployed in the South area of a BorderLayout, with the line:

```
Temp = new Scrollbar(Scrollbar.HORIZONTAL, 0, 20, -50, 150);
```

The arguments specify that this scrollbar is horizontal, its starting value (position of slider) is 0, the slider should occupy 20 pixels, the minimum value represented should be –50 and the maximum, 150.

The remaining components are deployed on their own panel which takes up the rest of the area. Scrollbar events are handled by **handleEvent(Event e)** not by **action(Event e, Object o)**. We use the Event Handler to trap the value of the scrollbar, and pass it to **convert(int x)** which processes the placing of new text into the TextFields.

```
import java.applet.Applet;
import java.awt.*;

public class myScroll extends Applet
{
    Panel p;
    Scrollbar Temp;
    Label CentLabel, FarLabel;
    TextField Centin, Farout;
    int f, c, answer;

    public void init( )
    {
        // Declare Layout Manager
        setLayout(new BorderLayout( ));
```

```
      Temp = new Scrollbar(Scrollbar.HORIZONTAL, 0, 20, -50,150);
      CentLabel = new Label("Degrees Centigrade");
      FarLabel = new Label("Degrees Fahrenheit");
      Centin = new TextField (5);
      Farout = new TextField(5);
      setBackground(Color.lightGray);

      p = new Panel( );
      p.add(CentLabel);
      p.add(Centin);
      p.add(FarLabel);
      p.add(Farout);

      add("Center", p);
      add("South", Temp);

      // set initial values in textFields
      Centin.setText("0");
      Farout.setText("32");
}

// simple conversion routine, takes Cent, returns Far.
public int calc(int x)
{
      answer=(((9 * x)/5) + 32 );
      return answer;
}

/* this method receives its argument from the scrollbar puts the
      value into the Centigrade box, calls calc( ) to do the sums
      and puts the result into the Farenheit box */
public void convert(int x)
{
      Centin.setText(Integer.toString(x));
      f = calc(x );
      Farout.setText( Integer.toString( f ));
}

// catches scrollbar events
public boolean handleEvent(Event e)
{
      int Scroll;
      if (e.target instanceof Scrollbar)
      {
```

```
        if (e.target == Temp)
        {
            Scroll = Temp.getValue( );
            convert(Scroll);
        }
    }
    return super.handleEvent(e);
  }
}
```

Methods available to Scrollbar include **getValue( )** used here, **setValue( )** which would allow the user to type values directly into the textField and see them reflected in the position of the Scrollbox. **setLineIncrement( )**, **getLineIncrement( )**, **setPageIncrement( )**, and **getPageIncrement( )**.

--------- # 8.5 Dialog boxes ---------

Dialog boxes are pop-up boxes which are used in one of two modes, both of which will be familiar to Windows users. The first mode is known as modal – this is the box that will not allow the user to do anything until they have dealt with the dialog box – an example of this is the warning box which appears if you try to save a file whose name is being used already. The second is known as modeless, and this is the one that can be found in the *About* menu of most software programs.

A dialog box

This code produces the modeless box shown above, notice that the **WINDOW_DESTROY** event in the dialog box code uses the **dispose( )**, **hide( )** methods, instead of **System.exit(0)** which would shut down the applet.

```java
import java.awt.*;

public class myDialog extends Frame
{
    public myDialog( )
    {
        // names the applet
        super("About Menu");

        // Create menubar to hold menu
        MenuBar mb = new MenuBar( );

        // Create HelpMenu
        Menu H = new Menu("Help");
        H.add(new MenuItem("About"));

        // use setHelpMenu to ensure rightmost position
        mb.setHelpMenu(H);

        // add Help menu to menubar
        mb.add(H);
        setMenuBar(mb);
        setBackground(Color.lightGray);
    }
    public boolean action(Event e, Object o)
    {
        // instantiates AboutBox object when menu item is selected
        if (e.target instanceof MenuItem)
        {
            if(o.equals("About"))
            {
                // pass the box a reference to this applet
                AboutBox a = new AboutBox(this);
                a.show( );
            }
        }
        return true;
    }
```

```java
public boolean handleEvent(Event e)
{
    if (e.id == Event.WINDOW_DESTROY)
    {
        System.exit(0);
        return true;
    }
    return super.handleEvent(e);
}

public static void main(String[] args)
{
    Frame f = new myDialog( );
    f.pack( );
    f.show( );
}
}
// define new class  for Dialog box
class AboutBox extends Dialog
{
    Label l, l1;
    Button b;
    Panel p, p1;
    myDialog parent;

    // constructor of the dialog box, receives object of type
    //  Frame ie. myDialog
    public AboutBox(Frame parent)
    {
        // false sets mode to modeless
        super( parent, "About TYJ", false);

        p = new Panel( );
        l = new Label("Teach Yourself Java");
        l1 = new Label("by Chris Wright");
        p.add(l);
        p.add(l1);

        b = new Button("OK");
        p1 = new Panel( );
```

```
    p1.add(b);

    add("Center", p);
    add("South", p1);
    pack( );
    show( );
}

public boolean handleEvent( Event e)
{
    if (e.id == Event.WINDOW_DESTROY)
    {
        // we don't want to shut down the applet!
        hide( );
        dispose( );
    }
    return super.handleEvent(e);
}

public boolean action(Event e, Object o)
{
    /* we only have one button in this program, so if it is a
       button it is the right button! */
    if (e.target instanceof Button)
    {
        hide( );
        dispose( );
    }
    return true;
}
}
```

──────8.6 Event handling in JDK 1.1──────

The event model we have used so far assumes that all events
will be trapped by a method in which a series of alternatives are
suggested, depending on what the target of the action is. Although
this is simple from the programmer's point of view, it does make

for complexity if the interface is anything more than simple. The way that events are handled in JDK1.1 is a radical departure in that we can now assign a listening object to anything in our class that will trigger an event. Different categories of objects trigger different types of event. This means the code that deals with an event is now bound directly to the specific object, instead of being part of the containing classes' **action( )** method.

The presence of this new event model does not mean that the old one will no longer work – it does – but learning the new one is advisable because it does represent a substantial improvement. In the new model, every type of event is represented by one of a number of Java classes. These classes are imported from the Java AWT with this statement:

```
import java.awt.event.*;
```

Let's take a look at a simple example of the new model in action.

```
import java.awt.*;
import java.awt.event.*;
import java.applet.Applet;

//We are going to implement the ActionListener interface
public class myNewButton extends Applet implements
ActionListener
{
   Button b;
   TextField t;
   int num, result;

   public void init( )
   {
      b = new Button("Double");

      /* now associate the ActionListener with the button using
         supplied method   */
      b.addActionListener(this);      //this refers to myButton class

      t = new TextField(7);
      t.setText("100");

      add(b);
      add(t);
   }
```

```
    // ActionListener has only one method - actionPerformed,
    // which we must implement
    public void actionPerformed( ActionEvent e)
    {
    num = Integer.parseInt(t.getText());
    result = num * 2;
    t.setText( Integer.toString(result));
    }
}
```

In this example we are implementing the ActionListener interface
which has only one method – **ActionPerformed(Event e)**.
There is nothing untoward about this, in fact it looks remarkably
similar to the old model, but slightly more concise – we do not
have to test whether the event is a button or not.

What happens if we have more than one button? Simple – any
component that generates an **ActionEvent** (Button, List, Menu-
Item or TextField), can be assigned to an **ActionListener**. The
ActionEvent can use the **getActionCommand( )** method to
obtain the action command string. If no string has been explicitly
set, then it simply returns the **Label** of the component. Now
that we can tell which component was responsible for the
ActionEvent, we can write appropriate code to deal with it.

```
import java.awt.*;
import java.awt.event.*;
import java.applet.Applet;

public class myNewTwoButtons extends Applet
    implements ActionListener
{
    Button b, b1;
    TextField t;
    int num, result;

    public void init( )
    {
        b = new Button("Double");
        b.addActionListener(this);
        // set tag for Action Listener to recognise button b by.
        b.setActionCommand("2");
        b1 = new Button("Treble");
```

```
        // the code doesn't require a tag, but it works both ways!
        b1.addActionListener(this);
        t = new TextField(7);
        t.setText("100");

        add(b);
        add(t);
        add(b1);
    }
    public void actionPerformed(ActionEvent e)
    {
    num = Integer.parseInt(t.getText( ));
    String s = e.getActionCommand( );
    if (s == ("2"))
    {
       result = num * 2;
    }
    else if (s == ("Treble"))
       {
           result = num * 3;
       }
    t.setText(Integer.toString(result));
    }
  }
```

ActionListener is probably the most useful class provided in the new event model, and it is convenient to use it as it only has one method for us to implement. However the AWT provides other classes with other interfaces such as **WindowListener** and **MouseListener**, both of which will be useful, but may have more methods than we actually need. We can skate around this problem by implementing the methods as skeletons containing no code, but this will require tedious and repetitive work and will make the program larger and harder to understand. Fortunately Java provides an *adapter* class for each interface that contains more than one method. This class implicitly implements empty versions of all the methods. To use an adapter class, we create a subclass of it, thus inheriting all the methods. This however is very limiting, as Java does not allow multiple inheritance – nearly all of the examples in this book extend one class or another. This precludes use of this technique for all but

a very few programs. A solution to this problem is to use a new
Java feature – Inner Classes.

Inner classes

Inner classes give us a way of using the adapter class, by nesting
it inside the class we are writing, in the form of a local class or
an anonymous class. This example represents the simple program
from the last section, using a local class.

```
import java.awt.*;
import java.awt.event.*;
import java.applet.Applet;

public class myLocalButton extends Applet
{
    private ActionListener al;
    private Button b;
    private TextField t;
    private int num, result;

    public void init( )
    {
        b = new Button("Double");
        al = new buttonListener( );
        b.addActionListener(al);
        t = new TextField(7);
        t.setText("100");

        add(b);
        add(t);
    }

    class buttonListener implements ActionListener
    {
        public void actionPerformed(ActionEvent e)
        {
        num = Integer.parseInt(t.getText());
        result = num * 2;
        t.setText( Integer.toString(result));
        }
    }
}
```

The container class declares an instance of the 'helper' class. Because it is contained in the **myLocalButton** class, the local class **buttonListener** enjoys the same access to methods and variables as any of the outer classes methods. Here the local class manipulates the private variables of the outer class directly.

Even more concise, and ideal for classes that do not contain large quantities of code, is the concept of *anonymous* classes. These are defined by an expression, which means that they can be included within an assignment or a call to a method.

```
import java.awt.*;
import java.awt.event.*;
import java.applet.Applet;

public class myNewInnerButton extends Applet
{
    Button b;
    TextField t;
    int num, result;

    public void init( )
    {
        b = new Button("Double");
        /* declare and define anonymous inner class, notice that the
           opening bracket before new is not closed until the end
           of the class definition contained in curly brackets.*/

        b.addActionListener(new ActionListener( ){
            public void actionPerformed(ActionEvent e)
            {
                num = Integer.parseInt(t.getText( ));
                result = num * 2;
                t.setText( Integer.toString(result));
            }
        }); // close both sets of brackets here, class and method call

        t = new TextField(7);
        t.setText("100");

        add(b);
        add(t);
    }
}
```

Having kept rigidly to a set style of indentation and bracketing, at first glance the anonymous class does little to enhance the readability of our code, however it has two major benefits, firstly it is very concise and secondly it allows us to bind the event handling of an object to the point of addition. This makes the logic of the program a great deal easier to follow. An effective strategy for dealing with anonymous classes is to have them call methods from the outer class. For example, this definition could have been written with a call to a method **calc(int x)** which would have contained the few lines of code required to perform the calculation on integer x.

Compile these programs and take a look at the directory listing, you will see that the compiler has produced a class for each inner class, in addition to the outer class.

We will now take a look at some of our earlier examples, rewritten to illustrate the handling of the type of event generated by different GUI components.

────8.7 Window events in 1.1────

You will recall that when we were working with an application, the closing of the window had to be handled in a **handleEvent()** method. In 1.1, a window event is handled by **WindowListener** which has seven methods:

```
windowActivated(WindowEvent)
windowClosed(WindowEvent)
windowClosing(WindowEvent)
windowDeactivated(WindowEvent)
windowDeiconified(WindowEvent)
windowIconified(WindowEvent)
windowOpened(WindowEvent)
```

This makes it a candidate to have its own adapter class – **WindowAdapter**. The following code demonstrates the use of the **WindowAdapter** interface, with **WindowClosing( )** implemented. Notice that the code to close the window (in function **close( )**), is shorter, because we no longer need to pass unhandled events back to the super class for reassignment. **WindowAdapter** will never know about the **Button** event that does the same job, because **Button** uses **ActionListener** to handle its events.

```java
import java.awt.*;
import java.awt.event.*;

public class myWindowEvent extends Frame
{
   private Button b;                // constructor for class
   public myWindowEvent( )
   {
     // create button and attach ActionListener
     b = new Button("Quit");
     b.addActionListener(new ActionListener( ){
       public void actionPerformed(ActionEvent e)
       {
       close( );
       }
     });
     // we still need to handle the Window Event, but we don't
     // want to implement all seven methods, so we use
     // WindowAdapter
     this.addWindowListener(new WindowAdapter( ){
       public void windowClosing(WindowEvent e)
       {
       close( );
       }
     });

     add(b);
     }

   // method used by both listeners!
   public void close( )
   {
     System.exit(0);
   }

   public static void main(String[ ] args)
   {
     Frame f = new myWindowEvent( );
```

```
    // resize is deprecated under 1.1, so use pack( ) instead
    f.pack( );
    f.show( );
  }
}
```

————8.8 Menu events in 1.1————

MenuItem triggers action events in the same way as a **Button**, but **CheckboxMenuItem** triggers item events only, using **Item-Listener** with its one method, **itemStateChanged(ItemEvent)**. We use **setState( )** and **getState( )** from **checkboxMenuItem** to find out whether the option has been checked.

This code demonstrates the use of menus with 1.1, using anonymous classes. The program is a version of the Breakfast example seen earlier. It prints your choice to the System window.

```java
import java.awt.*;
import java.awt.event.*;
import java.io.*;

public class myMenuEvent extends Frame
{
   private Button b;
   private MenuItem wheat, bacon, eggs, toast;
   private CheckboxMenuItem hot, iced;

   public myMenuEvent( )
   {
      setLayout(new BorderLayout(20,20));

      // Add button and look after window closing
      b = new Button("Quit");
      b.addActionListener(new ActionListener( ){
        public void actionPerformed(ActionEvent e)
        {
        System.exit(0);
        }
      });
```

```
this.addWindowListener(new WindowAdapter( ){
   public void windowClosing(WindowEvent e)
   {
   System.exit(0);
   }
});

// for clarity set up menu first then listeners!
MenuBar mb = new MenuBar();
this.setMenuBar(mb);
Menu Breakfast = new Menu("Breakfast");
Menu coffee = new Menu("Coffee");
mb.add(Breakfast);
Breakfast.add(wheat = new MenuItem("Cereal"));
Breakfast.add(bacon = new MenuItem("Rashers"));
Breakfast.add(eggs = new MenuItem("Eggs"));
   // coffee is clickable submenu
   coffee.add(hot = new CheckboxMenuItem("Hot"));
   coffee.add(iced = new CheckboxMenuItem("Iced"));
Breakfast.add(coffee);
Breakfast.add(toast = new MenuItem("Toast"));

// now do all the listeners!
wheat.addActionListener(new ActionListener( ){
   public void actionPerformed(ActionEvent e)
   {
      message("Cereal");
   }
});

bacon.addActionListener(new ActionListener( ){
   public void actionPerformed(ActionEvent e)
   {
      message("Rashers");
   }
});

eggs.addActionListener(new ActionListener( ){
   public void actionPerformed(ActionEvent e)
   {
      message("Eggs");
   }
});
```

```java
      toast.addActionListener(new ActionListener( ){
        public void actionPerformed(ActionEvent e)
        {
            message("Toast");
        }
      });

      // set state of other option to unchecked if hot is chosen,
      // you cannot have iced hot coffee!
      hot.addItemListener(new ItemListener( ){
        public void itemStateChanged(ItemEvent e)
        {
            if(hot.getState( )==true)
               message("Hot Coffee");
            iced.setState(false);
        }
      });

      // use getState to see if it has been clicked on or off
      iced.addItemListener(new ItemListener( ){
        public void itemStateChanged(ItemEvent e)
        {
            if(iced.getState( )==true)
            message("Iced Coffee");
            hot.setState(false);
        }
      });

      add(b);
      }

      // you didn't expect a cooked breakfast did you?
      void message(String s)
      {
         System.out.println("You have chosen: " + s);
      }

      public static void main(String[ ] args)
      {
         Frame f = new myMenuEvent( );
         f.pack( );
         f.show( );
      }

}
```

8.9 Dialog events in 1.1

There are no specific events associated uniquely with dialog boxes. They are created in response to an **actionEvent** triggered by a button or menuItem. Using dialog boxes with inner classes does provide one interesting point.

The most notable thing about dialog boxes in 1.1 is the problem posed by the presence of the inner class that deals with the menu item invoking the dialog box. The invocation we used before (page 155) was:

```
a = new AboutBox(this);
a.show( );
```

The problem is caused by the presence of **this** as a paremeter. Because it is part of an inner class, the **this** that is referred to is of course the inner class, which is not an extension of **Frame**. The problem is solved by rewriting the invocation thus:

```
a = new AboutBox(myNewDialog.this);
a.show( );
```

This is the code for the complete program.

```
import java.awt.*;
import java.awt.event.*;

public class myNewDialog extends Frame
{
   private Button b;
   private MenuItem about;
   private About a;

   public myNewDialog( )
   {
     setLayout(new BorderLayout(20,20));
     b = new Button("Quit");
     b.addActionListener(new ActionListener( ){
       public void actionPerformed(ActionEvent e)
       {
          System.exit(0);
       }
     });
```

```java
    this.addWindowListener(new WindowAdapter( ){
      public void windowClosing(WindowEvent e)
      {
        System.exit(0);
      }
    });

    MenuBar mb = new MenuBar( );
    this.setMenuBar(mb);
    Menu Help = new Menu("Help");
    mb.add(Help);
    Help.add(about = new MenuItem("About"));

    about.addActionListener(new ActionListener( ){
      public void actionPerformed(ActionEvent e)
      {
        a = new About(myNewDialog.this);
        a.show( );
      }
    });

    add(b);
  }

  public static void main(String[ ] args)
  {
    Frame f = new myNewDialog( );
    f.pack( );
    f.show( );
  }
}

class AboutBox extends Dialog
{
    private Button b;
    private Label l, l1;
    private Panel p, p1;

    public About(Frame parent)
    {
      super(parent, "About", false);
      b = new Button("OK");
      p = new Panel( );
      p1 = new Panel( );
      l = new Label("Teach Yourself Java");
```

```
      l1 = new Label("Chris Wright");

      p.add(l);
      p.add(l1);
      p1.add(b);

      b.addActionListener(new ActionListener( ){
        public void actionPerformed(ActionEvent e)
        {
        dispose( );
        }
      });

      this.addWindowListener(new WindowAdapter( ){
        public void windowClosing(WindowEvent e)
        {
        dispose( );
        }
      });

      add("Center", p);
      add("South", b);
      pack( );
      show( );
    }
  }
```

————8.10 Mouse events in 1.1————

Mouse Events are provided with two adapter classes, **MouseAdapter** and **MouseMotionAdapter**.

The Listener methods provided by the **MouseAdapter** class are **mouseClicked( )** where the user has pressed and released the button on a component without moving it, **mouseEntered( )** where the mouse pointer crosses the border of a component, **mouseExited( )** where the mouse pointer leaves a component, **mousePressed( )** where the mouse is 'clicked and dragged', and **mouseReleased( )** where the pressed button is released.

The **mouseMotionAdapter** class provides us with **mouseDragged( )** which deals with events caused by 'clicking and dragging' and **mouseMoved( )**, which deals with events caused by moving the mouse without clicking.

This program draws a line on the applet panel, whilst echoing the mouse coordinates to the staus bar. We will use **mousePressed( )** to let us know where to start drawing, and **mouseDragged( )** to record the successive x,y coordinates. Note that we require our graphics context to be the applet, not the inner class.

```
Graphics g = myNewCoordinates.this.getGraphics( );
```

This line uses the same technique as the Dialog box program to ensure that the graphics context is the applet.

This is the complete code for the program.

```
import java.awt.*;
import java.awt.event.*;
import java.applet.Applet;

public class myNewCoordinates extends Applet
{
    private int lastX, lastY;
    private Color myColor = Color.blue;

    public void init( )
    {
        this.setBackground(Color.red);
        this.addMouseListener(new MouseAdapter( ){
            public void mousePressed(MouseEvent e)
            {
            lastX = e.getX( );
            lastY = e.getY( );
            }
        });

        this.addMouseMotionListener(new MouseMotionAdapter( ){
            public void mouseDragged(MouseEvent e)
            {
                Graphics g = myNewCoordinates.this.getGraphics( );
                g.setColor(myColor);
                int x = e.getX( );
                int y = e.getY( );
                g.drawLine(lastX, lastY, x, y);
```

```
        lastX = x;
        lastY = y;
        showStatus("Mouse is at: ( " + lastX + "," + lastY+ ")");
      } // end mouseDragged
   }); // end inner class
 } // end init( )

} // end class definition
```

————8.11 Scrollbar events in 1.1————

Scrollbar events are trapped by an **AdjustmentListener** which has one method, **adjustmentValueChanged( )**. We can place the code that records the new scrollbar value inside this method.

This is the complete code for the temperature conversion program.

```
import java.applet.Applet;
import java.awt.*;
import java.awt.event.*;

public class myInnerScroll extends Applet
{
   Private Panel p;
   Private Scrollbar Temp;
   Private Label CentLabel, FarLabel;
   Private TextField Centin, Farout;
   Private int f, c, answer;

   public void init( )
   {
      setLayout(new BorderLayout( ));

      Temp = new Scrollbar(Scrollbar.HORIZONTAL, 0, 20, -50, 150);
      Temp.addAdjustmentListener(new AdjustmentListener( ){
         public void adjustmentValueChanged(AdjustmentEvent e)
         {
            int Scroll;
            Scroll = Temp.getValue( );
            convert(Scroll);
         }
      });
```

```java
        CentLabel = new Label("Degrees Centigrade");
        FarLabel = new Label("Degrees Fahrenheit");
        Centin = new TextField (5);
        Farout = new TextField(5);
        setBackground(Color.lightGray);

        p = new Panel( );
        p.add(CentLabel);
        p.add(Centin);
        p.add(FarLabel);
        p.add(Farout);

        add("Center", p);
        add("South", Temp);
        Centin.setText("0");
        Farout.setText("32");
    }
    public int calc(int x)
    {
        answer=(((9 * x)/5) + 32);
        return answer;
    }

    public void convert(int x)
    {
        System.out.println("Temp Centigrade is: " + x);
        Centin.setText(Integer.toString(x));
        f = calc(x);
        Farout.setText( Integer.toString(f));
    }
}
```

8.12 Summary

This chapter is by no means a complete guide to the new event model, but is intended to demonstrate ways in which we can use the new event model in our programs. For full documentation refer to the online resources, listed at the end of this book.

The advantages the new event model brings are clarity, conciseness and economy of processing. We are now able to write our event handling code at the same time as we add the components to the program, making the process more intuitive.

The introduction of inner classes has greater implications. It enables us to bundle 'helper' classes with the class that they help, without going through the tortuous process of explicitly telling each class which other classes it knows about. This certainly makes working with classes a more intuitive process and should therefore enable us to increase our productivity. From the beginner's point of view, it does increase the complexity of the object model, especially as it effectively gives us a hierarchy of containment as well as one of inheritance.

While every programmer establishes a method of working which is informed by their understanding of the language, and by the types of application that they are used to creating, I would suggest that a good way to approach inner classes is only to use them where the class is specifically designed to be bundled with one and only one application. If the class can be abstracted into a state where it might be reused in another application, such as the keyboard class in our calculator application, then it should be left as a standalone class. Using inner classes to deal with the event handling of an application is a good example of this kind of application specific behaviour.

————— 8.13 Exercises —————

1. Rewrite the calculator program so it becomes a free floating window that can be opened by clicking a button in an applet.

2. Write an application that allows the user to write in a TextField. Menus should be available to allow the user to change Font, Style and Size.

3. Rewrite the Temperature Conversion program so that it is available as a pop-upwindow from an applet button.

4. Write an application, using JDK 1.1 event handling that allows the user to draw a picture on a canvas. There should be a menu system allowing the user to select different colours.

9

INPUT/OUTPUT AND COMMUNICATIONS

——— 9.1 Aims of this chapter ———

The aim of this chapter is to examine very briefly how Java handles input and output at a local level in order to familiarise ourselves with basic principles and then to look in greater depth at Internet level communications. We will look at file handling (restricted in Java to applications), and at the way Java uses Stream classes for data transfer. At Internet level we will look at the concept of protocols, examining **http**, and **tcp** and **ip**. We shall examine the classes provided by **java.net** and create a simple client and server as a demonstration of these classes. Finally we shall create a text-based browser, using the new character based stream classes supplied with Java 1.1.

——9.2 Introducing I/O and networking——

Input/Output, or I/O as it is usually referred to, refers to the methods a computer uses to read data in (Input) from an external source such as a keyboard or a file, and to write data out (Output) to an external source such as a monitor or a file. This model can be logically extended to include other computers and other networks. The Internet is an example of computers reading and writing to other computers on other networks.

Java 1.0 provides us with an attractively intuitive method of handling data transfer, with its use of byte **Stream** classes, the most important of which are:

InputStream	OutputStream
BufferedInputStream	BufferedOutputStream
DataInputStream	DataOutputStream
FileInputStream	FileOutputStream
StringBufferInputStream	PrintStream

The disadvantage inherant in the use of byte-based classes for data transfer is that it does not handle text particularly efficiently, notably text containing symbols from an extended character set such as Cyrillic, or Japanese, which will require more than one byte for certain characters.

Java 1.1 provides an analogous set of character based input and output streams to deal with textual I/O, which are extended from **Reader** and **Writer** respectively. They are more efficient than byte streams and because they convert characters into Unicode (using two bytes) for internal handling, are ideal for implementing internationalised programs, where character sets may prove problematic for byte stream implementations.

BufferedReader	BufferedWriter
LineNumberReader	StringWriter
CharArrayReader	CharArrayWriter
FilterReader	FilterWriter
PushBackReader	
InputStreamReader	OutputStreamWriter
FileReader	FileWriter
PipedReader	PrintWriter
StringReader	StringWriter

Although it is not necessary at this stage to know all the details of every class provided for I/O in Java, we will look at some of the classes we are likely to find useful in our programs.

—9.3 InputStream and OutputStream—

These two classes are abstract classes used as the base for the other stream classes. They provide an interface for reading and writing *bytes* of information.

How do they work?

All the programs we have written so far send a message to an object explicitly, by means of a function call. We obviously don't want to embed every part of every message we send along a cable inside that type of computer program – that would be wasteful. The solution to this quandry is that when we create an object of type **InputStream** we place it in an endless loop which only terminates when data becomes available. This has the effect of the InputStream listening and waiting for action on the line. This is known as *blocking*. When a signal is sent, the contents of the loop are invoked.

The most basic example of input and output in action is to read characters from the keyboard and write them to the screen. We need therefore to create a situation where the program listens for activity from the keyboard. This would be called *System input*.

The technique we use to create this listening loop requires *exception* handling, because we need to be able to escape from the loop if something goes wrong. An exception is *thrown* when a problem strikes. It is the programmer's job to catch these exceptions before they unexpectedly terminate the program. We can do this by creating a **try ... catch** loop.

```
try
    {
        // Some activity or other
    }
catch(Exception e)
    {
        // What we do when exception e occurs
    }
```

There are a number of known exceptions provided for in the language, these include **IOException**, which would be the one thrown here. All the known exceptions are subclasses of **java.lang.throwable**.

We have used output from the system frequently in example programs as a means of providing feedback to the screen, so it should come as no surprise that the standard input and output variables provided by the **System** class are **in** and **out**.

StringBuffer

The **StringBuffer** object allows us to add characters into an expandable buffer. The contents can be printed out again with a call to the System output stream **out**.

```java
import java.io.*;
class Keyboard
{
    public static void main(String[] args)
    {
        StringBuffer sb = new StringBuffer( );
        char c;
        try
        {
            // cast integer representation to char
            while ((c = (char)System.in.read( )) != '\n')
            {
                // add char to end of StringBuffer contents
                sb.append(c);
            }
        }
        catch(Exception e)
        {
            System.out.println("Exception: " + e.getMessage( ) + "has
                occurred");
        }
        System.out.println(sb);
    }
}
```

Once more the Java libraries make life simple. Here we are using the **StringBuffer** class to hold a variable sized string of characters, read in from the keyboard using the **InputStream** object **in**, terminated by the new line character (carriage return). The system reads the characters in from the keyboard, and when the user presses the Enter key, prints the contents of the StringBuffer to the screen, using the **OutputStream** object **out**. We need to catch the possibility of an I/O exception, so we place the reading in of characters within a **try...catch** loop. The actual exception would be relayed to the screen by the **Throwable** method **getMessage( )**.

FileOutputStream

If we wanted to write the stream in the previous program to a file, we would use **FileOutputStream(filename)**:

```
import java.io.*;
class myFile
{
   public static void main(String[ ] args)
   {
      StringBuffer sb = new StringBuffer( );
      char c;

      try
      {
         while ((c = (char)System.in.read( )) != '\n')
         {
            sb.append(c);
         }
      }
      catch(Exception e)
      {
         System.out.println("Exception: " + e.getMessage( ) + "has
            occurred");
      }

      /*  Now convert StringBuffer to a String and store in a byte
         Array, ready to pass to FileOutputStream. */
      String s = sb.toString( );
      byte[ ] buffer = new byte[64];
      s.getBytes(0, s.length(), buffer, 0);

      // create a file myFile.txt and write contents of buffer to it.
```

```
      try
      {
         FileOutputStream out = new FileOutputStream("myFile.txt");
         out.write(buffer);
      }
      catch(Exception e)
      {
         System.out.println("Exception: " + e.getMessage( ) + "has
                    occurred");
      }
   }
}
```

Had we known that we wanted the input saved in a file, rather
than printed to the screen,we could have saved ourselves the
trouble of converting the **stringBuffer**, and read it straight into
a byte array. This anomaly exists because the **System.out.
println( )** method takes a string as an argument, whereas the
FileOutputStream object takes a byte array, not a string.

This code fragment illustrates reading keyboard-generated text
straight into a byte array.

```
import java.io.*;
class myFile
{
   public static void main(String[ ] args)
   {
      byte[ ] buffer = new byte[64];
      try
      {
      // read into the beginning of our array – not over 64 bytes!
         System.in.read(buffer, 0, 64);
      }
      catch(Exception e)
      {
         System.out.println("Exception: " + e.getMessage( ) + "has
            occurred");
      }
```

Here we create a byte array of 64 bytes, and read into it from the
keyboard, specifying a zero offset (ie. beginning at location 0),
and a maximum of 64 bytes.

FileInputStream

To read from a file, we reverse the process.

```java
import java.io.*;
class myFile2
{
    public static void main(String[] args)
    {
        File f = new File("myFile.txt");
        int l = (int)f.length( );
        byte[ ] buffer = new byte[l];

        try
    {
        FileInputStream in = new FileInputStream("myFile.txt");
        in.read(buffer, 0, l);
    }
        catch(Exception e)
    {
        System.out.println("Exception: " + e.getMessage( ) + "has
            occurred");
    }

        String s = new String(buffer, 0);
        System.out.println(s)
    }
}
```

In this example, we check to find out how long the file is, create
a byte array of that length to hold it and read it into the array
using a **FileInputStream** object.

DataInputStream

DataInputStream is the class we will get most use out of,
because it contains methods that allow us to slurp up data in
usably large chunks – **readFully(byte Array)** and by the line
readLine( ), as well as by byte, **readByte( )** and by char,
readChar( ). We will use **readLine( )** to read text from the
keyboard into a String, using a **DataInputStream** object.

```
import java.io.*;
class Dinput
{
   public static void main(String[ ] args)
   {
      DataInputStream in = new DataInputStream(System.in);
      String s = new String( );

      try
      {
         s = in.readLine( );
      }
      catch(Exception e)
      {
         System.out.println("Exception: " + e.getMessage( ) + "has
            occurred");
      }

      System.out.println(s);
   }
}
```

It is worth noting at this point that the **readLine( )** method is deprecated in Java 1.1. The alternative is to use **read( )**, which returns an integer (**bytesRead**), to put the string into a byte array and then print it out to the screen.

——9.4 Messages to remote computers——

In principle, sending messages to remote computers is no more complicated than dealing with local I/O. The only complexity involved is in addressing the computer.

Every computer connected to the Internet has a unique IP (Internet Protocol) address. This is a sequence of four four-digit numbers describing the network the computer is part of, and the actual computer itself. This address is commonly represented as a *host name* – for example *chroma.demon.co.uk* represents the IP address of my computer. The computer requires the numerical version of the address for communication. It can get this by a process known as DNS lookup.

DNS lookup

Every network has access to a Domain Name Server. This computer keeps a list of known addresses and their numerical counterparts, allowing us to quiz DNS for the numerical data our program needs to connect to a server.

We will now write a simple program to discover the IP address of a known computer. The address supplied, *turnip.co.uk,* probably doesn't exist – supply your own details instead.

The class we will use to do this comes from **java.net** and is called **InetAddress**. This class provides a handy method called **getByName(String Hostname)**, which returns the IP address of the HostName.

```java
import java.net.*;

class hostName
{
    public static void main(String[] args)
    {
        try
        {
            // create an InetAddress object called host
            InetAddress host =InetAddress.getByName("turnip.co.uk");
            // print out the name and IP address
            System.out.println(host);
        }
        // since turnip.co.uk doesn't exist, we will need this catch!
        catch(UnknownHostException e)
        {
        System.out.println("Cannot find IP number");
        }
    }
}
```

We now know how to address a remote computer, and we know that the computer has to be listening for a communication, but how does it know which communication is which. After all, a Web server serves up thousands of pages daily, how will it deal with different kinds of request?

Obviously a server is not sitting waiting to process somebody else's keyboard strokes. To communicate between two computers, we need a software program dedicated to listening for a particular type of communication. We can write this ourselves, or we can make use of one of a number of well known programs that are resident on most Web servers, for example, **Echo**, which is used in the real world to test that a particular server is alive. The program does exactly what the programs we wrote earlier do – echoes the keyboard strokes back to the sending computer.

To differentiate between incoming signals, computers use a method involving *Ports* and *Sockets*.

Ports and Sockets

Every computer communicates through a virtual *port*. Ports are numbered and when we send a message to an Echo client, we address it to a particular port number (Echo = Port 7). When an Echo server listening on Port 7 receives a message from a remote computer, it creates a *socket* through which all subsequent communication is made, using the remote computer's IP address and port number as a unique identifier for the session. It then goes back to listening at the port for the next computer to make contact. While this is going on, it may also be listening on port 80 for HTTP requests for Web pages. A single port can create many sockets – in certain protocols, such as FTP, a second port is used to act as a control channel. This method is used by all computers and is why we can open several different Web pages simultaneously or download E-mail at the same time as Web pages. All these transactions will occur on different port numbers.

Protocols

A *protocol* in computer communications is an agreement between two ends of a communication that data will be treated in a certain way, and that the business of transferring the data will be carried out in a specified way. The Internet uses a number of protocols, the most familiar of which will be HTTP and FTP which are application layer protocols, or TCP and UDP which are transport layer protocols.

Other examples include SMTP and POP, the E-mail protocols, and IP, the Internet Protocol.

HTTP

HTTP or Hyper Text Transfer Protocol is the standard that specifies how communication occurs between a browser and a server, across the Internet. The prefix **http://** that is found at the beginning of a URL is no more than an instruction to the application that this is the protocol to be used. The command

http://www.unl.ac.uk/~cwright/java/browser.html

that is sent to a server requesting a Web page can be loosely translated as

GET using **http**, the page: **browser.html**; residing in the directory in the account of **cwright** at the **University of North London**.

The URL itself breaks down into a protocol specifier, **http:**, the address of a Web server, in this case the one at the University of North London, where I have an account, and the directory and filename requested. In response to such a request, the server sends a message containing the Response Code (usually 'OK'), the MIME type and length of file followed by the data contained in the file itself.

FTP

FTP (File Transfer Protocol) specifies how a file is transferred between two end points. This is used when a file is downloaded from the net, or when you upload Web pages to a server.

TCP

TCP (Transmission Control Protocol) is a stream based, connection oriented protocol that provides part of the delivery system of the Internet. Often messages from the application layer such as FTP will be encapsulated within a TCP segment which carries the port number of the other end point. This segment will be encapsulated within an IP packet which carries the Internet address of the remote computer.

IP

IP is a packet oriented, connectionless protocol that deals in computer to computer communication, combined with TCP, a message can be delivered to a specific port number on any computer attached to the Internet.

For an example, we are going to demonstrate the ease with which the Java stream paradigm can be used to perform TCP connections.

——————— 9.5 The Echo client ———————

The following program uses TCP, which is a stream oriented protocol used by nearly every Internet application. TCP works in the same way as a telephone call. A connection is made and communication happens across the connection for the duration of the call. This is why TCP is known as a connection oriented protocol. Briefly, TCP works by call and response – it sends a request to open a connection to the server on the specified port. The server acknowledges and the connection is opened. When data is sent using TCP, all the error checking is done by the protocol, so we don't need to check that the message is intact, all we need to do is to implement the data processing and the initial setting up of the connection.

We know how to address an application and a computer, and given that the Echo server is run on Port 7, we can write a client application to connect to an Echo server on a remote host. Because of the security restrictions on applets, if we wrote this program as an applet it would only be able to contact the server from which it is served. To keep things interesting, we will write these programs as applications.

The following program uses **DataInputStream** to read input from the keyboard and from the socket, and a **PrintStream** to write the data to the socket. The socket itself comes from the **Socket** class, which hides much of the complexity of network programming from us.

```java
import java.io.*;
import java.net.*;

public class EchoClient
{
    public static void main(String[ ] args)
    {
        // declare objects we require
        Socket  mySocket;
        DataInputStream in;
        DataInputStream kbdInput;
        // can't use DataOutputStream as we need a println method
        PrintStream out;
        String hostname;
        String s;

        hostname = "turnip.co.uk";

        try
        {
            /* create a socket connected to remote Port 7;
               DNS lookup is automatic */
            localSocket = new Socket (hostname, 7);

            // set up data streams in & out of socket and from keyboard
            in = new DataInputStream(mySocket.getInputStream());
            out = new PrintStream(mySocket.getOutputStream( ));
            kbdInput = new DataInputStream(System.in);

            // while we have a connection
            while (true)
            {
                // acknowledgement of connection request
                System.out.println(" Connection made with: " +
                    mySocket.getInetAddress( ) + "\nRemote Port: " +
                        mySocket.getPort( )+ "\nOn  Local Port: " +
                            mySocket.getLocalPort( ));
                // read keyboard to String
                s = kbdInput.readLine( );
                // no need to carry on if there is no input
                if (s == null) break;
                // print string to the socket for output
                out.println(s);
```

```
            //read incoming string from the socket
            System.out.println(in.readLine( ));
        }
    }
    catch (UnknownHostException e)
    {
        System.out.println(e.getMessage( ));
    }
    catch (IOException e)
    {
        System.out.println(e.getMessage( ));
    }
  }
}
```

The **Socket** method **getPort( )**, which we use to display the details of the transaction, returns the remote port. To find out what port the client program has used, we use **getLocalPort( )**.

It is important to realise that not all servers run the Echo program. If you have difficulty finding one that does, we can set up a server locally, just to demonstrate this program.

─────── 9.6 The Echo server ───────

This program is a bare-bones example, just to demonstrate the communication between processes. Firstly we need a different kind of **Socket**, a **serverSocket**. **serverSocket** takes a port number as an argument and simply listens at that port for communication. We create a **serverSocket** on port 9999. This number is guaranteed to be unused – it is not allocated to any known program.

This arrangement requires that the client program must be modified to connect to hostname '*localhost*' on port 9999. The hostname 'localhost' returns the address 127.0.0.1 which means 'this computer'. It causes the message to be looped back to the same computer it originated from and is commonly used to test communications programs.

Once the **serverSocket** has been set up, we listen at port 9999 for a message. When one arrives we set up a socket to deal with it with the line

```
clientSocket = echoServer.accept( );
```

allowing the **serverSocket** to return to listening. Having set up the socket, we need to process the data. Because the function of the program is merely to echo the data back to the sender, all we need is to set up a single **dataInputStream** to handle the incoming traffic and a **PrintStream**. Once we have done this, we simply write the incoming data straight to the socket.

```
s = in.readLine( );
out.println(s);
```

Note that this server will accept connections from remote machines, but it will not deal with more than one connection at a time unless we create a separate thread for the server to run new sockets in.

```
import java.io.*;
import java.net.*;

public class EchoServer
{
    public static void main(String[] args)
    {
        // declare local variables
        ServerSocket echoServer = null;
        Socket clientSocket = null;
        DataInputStream in;
        PrintStream out;
        String s;
        // fire up server, catching IOException in case of problems
        try
        {
            echoServer = new ServerSocket(9999);
        }
        catch (IOException e)
        {
            System.out.println(e.getMessage( ));
        }
        if (echoServer != null)
```

```
        {
            System.out.println(" EchoServer listening on port 9999");
        }
        // create a new socket for incoming transactions and
        // Streams to handle data
        try
        {
            clientSocket = echoServer.accept( );
            in = new DataInputStream(clientSocket.getInputStream( ));
            out = new PrintStream(clientSocket.getOutputStream( ));
            // if socket created, print out details
            while (true)
            {
                System.out.println("Message Received From: " +
                    clientSocket.getInetAddress() + "\nFrom Port: " +
                        clientSocket.getPort( ));
                // send input to output!
                s = in.readLine( );
                out.println(s);
            }
        }
        catch (IOException e)
        {
            System.out.println(e.getMessage( ));
        }
    }
}
```

Multi Threaded Echo Server

To make this program more lifelike, we need it to be able to
handle multiple connections, to create a number of sockets and
process the transaction for each one. To make this possible we
need to have both the **serverSocket** and the transaction
processing run in their own threads. As the class does not extend
any other class, we can simply subclass **Thread** directly. Notice
how the initialisation is placed in the constructor for the class,
the work is done by the **run( )** method.

We actually create two separate classes in this program. The
Transaction class does all the data processing. A new instance
of **Transaction** is created for each connection and run in a

separate thread. The computer runs both classes simultaneously.

```java
import java.io.*;
import java.net.*;

public class ThreadEchoServer extends Thread
{
    /* declare classes - if we wanted to extend this class, private
    should be changed to protected so that the subclass can
    access these objects.*/
    private ServerSocket echoServer = null;
    private Socket clientSocket = null;

    // constructor sets up server and calls start( ) method of thread
    public ThreadEchoServer( )
    {
        try
        {
            echoServer = new ServerSocket(9999);
        }
        catch (IOException e)
        {
            System.out.println(e.getMessage( ));
        }
        System.out.println("EchoServer listening on port 9999");
        this.start( );
    }

    // this part will be run in as many threads as we have connections
    public void run( )
    {
        int i = 1;
        try
        {
            while(true)
            {
                clientSocket = echoServer.accept( );
                // hand over processing to new transaction object
                Transaction t = new Transaction(clientSocket);
                // print out a number for this transaction
                System.out.println("Transaction: "+ i + " created");
                i++;
            }
        }
```

```
      catch (IOException e)
      {
         System.out.println(e.getMessage( ));
      }
   }

   // instantiate object
   public static void main(String[ ] args)
   {
      new ThreadEchoServer( );
   }

}

// this class handles the actual data processing
class Transaction extends Thread
{
   private Socket client;
   private DataInputStream in;
   private PrintStream out;

   // constructor to initialise objects
   public Transaction(Socket clientSocket)
   {
      client = clientSocket;
      try
      {
         in = new DataInputStream(client.getInputStream( ));
         out = new PrintStream(client.getOutputStream( ));
      }
      catch(IOException e)
      {
         System.out.println(e.getMessage( ));
      }
      this.start( );
   }

   // run method handles the data
   public void run( )
   {
      String s;
      try
      {
         while (true)
```

```
        {
            System.out.println("Message Received From: " +
                client.getInetAddress(+ "\nFrom Port: " +
                    client.getPort( ));

            s = in.readLine( );
            out.println(s);
        }
    }
    catch(IOException e)
    {
        System.out.println(e.getMessage( ));
    }
  }
}
```

Now that we have an application that can send and receive messages across the Internet, we can go on to something a little more interesting– retrieving data from the Internet using HTTP.

————9.7 The HTTP client————

HTTP, or Hyper Text Transfer Protocol, is the means by which Web browsers download Web pages from the Internet. It is not terribly difficult in Java to write a simple client that provides the basic functionality of a Web browser by downloading text / HTML files from the Internet, and reporting the status of the transaction back to the user with the response from the server. We can also use the **java.net** package to find out the content type of the file, its length and the date it was last modified.

This program is an application, because an application allows us to contact any server on the Internet. It is written using the **HttpURLConnection** class which is only available in JDK 1.1. This class is a specialised version of **URLConnection**, and allows us to trap the response from the HTTP server at the other end of the connection, in addition to finding out data about the file we are downloading. As we are only interested in text, we will use the character based I/O streams from **java.io**. We will also use anonymous Innerclasses to deal with our event handling.

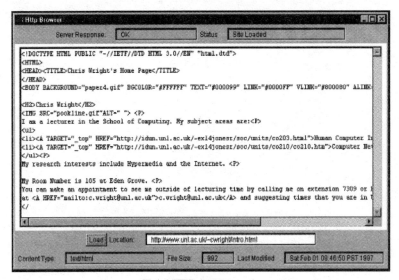

The HTTP browser

The user types a URL into the location field and clicks on the 'Load' button. The Java classes save us from coding the fine details of the transaction, but they do allow us to trap some information about the file. This can be displayed in TextFields.

```java
import java.io.*;
import java.net.*;
import java.awt.*;
import java.awt.event.*;
import java.util.*;         // required to manipulate Date

class Browser extends Frame
{
    // declare all HCI elements
    private Label locLabel, responseLabel,statusLabel,
        typeLabel, sizeLabel, modifiedLabel;
    private TextField locDisplay, response, status, contentType,
        size, modified;
    private Button b;
    private TextArea display;

    // construct object - ready for action
```

```
public Browser( )
{
    setTitle("Http Browser");

    Panel p = new Panel();

    p.setLayout(new BorderLayout());

        Panel pa = new Panel();
        pa.setBackground(Color.lightGray);
        responseLabel = new Label("Server Response: ");
        response = new TextField(20);
        response.setEditable(false);
        statusLabel = new Label("Status");
        status = new TextField(30);
        pa.add(responseLabel);
        pa.add(response);
        pa.add(statusLabel);
        pa.add(status);

        Panel pb = new Panel();
        display = new TextArea(20, 100);
        Font f = new Font("Courier", Font.PLAIN, 12);
        display.setFont(f);
        display.setEditable(false);
        pb.add(display);

    p.add("North", pa);
    p.add("Center", pb);

    Panel p1 = new Panel( );
    b = new Button("Load");
    b.addActionListener(new ActionListener( ){
        public void actionPerformed(ActionEvent e)
        {
            retrieve( );
        }
    });

    locLabel = new Label("Location: ");
    locDisplay = new TextField(45);

    p1.setBackground(Color.lightGray);
    p1.add(b);
    p1.add(locLabel);
```

```
    p1.add(locDisplay);

    Panel p2 = new Panel( );
    typeLabel = new Label("Content Type: ");
    contentType = new TextField(25);
    contentType.setEditable(false);
    sizeLabel = new Label("File Size: ");
    size = new TextField(6);
    size.setEditable(false);
    modifiedLabel = new Label("Last Modified");
    modified = new TextField(25);
    modified.setEditable(false);

    p2.setBackground(Color.lightGray);
    p2.add(typeLabel);
    p2.add(contentType);
    p2.add(sizeLabel);
    p2.add(size);
    p2.add(modifiedLabel);
    p2.add(modified);

    add("North", p);
    add("Center", p1);
    add("South", p2);

    // Not forgetting to allow the user to close the window!
    this.addWindowListener(new WindowAdapter( ){
       public void windowClosing(WindowEvent e)
       {
          System.exit(0);
       }
    });
}

// how it works!
public void retrieve( )
{
    // declare local variables - not to be used outside this method
    URL target = null;
    String contents = null;
    String type = null;
    String server = null;
    Date date = null;
```

```java
int length = 0;

// start the loop
try
{
    // read in the users text from the location field
    target = new URL(locDisplay.getText( ));

    // let user know that we are doing something!
    status.setText("Finding: "+ target);

    // initialise an HttpURLConnection object when
    // connection  is available
    HttpURLConnection fetch =
        (HttpURLConnection)target.openConnection( );

    // use HttpURLConnection object to get server response
    server = fetch.getResponseMessage( );

    // pass server response message to display for user
    response.setText(server);

    // read a character based input stream directly into
    // BufferedReader
    BufferedReader in = new BufferedReader(new
        InputStreamReader(fetch.getInputStream( )));

    // Let user know that we are receiving data
    status.setText("Loading Pages now...");
    display.setText("");

    // prepare a character array to hold 1Kb of data from
    // Buffered Reader
    char[ ] buffer = new char[1024];
    int charsRead;

    // read it in from BufferedReader to character array
    while((charsRead = in.read(buffer, 0, 1024)) != -1)
    {
        // put character data into a String and display
        contents = new String(buffer, 0, charsRead);
        display.append(contents);
    }
```

```
    /* leaving this loop requires in.read( ) to return -1, which
    implies there is no  more data being transferred so
    we assume that all the text has been transferred */
    status.setText("Site Loaded");

    // interrogate inputstream headers
    type = fetch.getContentType( );
    length = fetch.getContentLength( );
    date = new Date(fetch.getLastModified( ));

    // print information to appropriate textField
    contentType.setText(type);
    size.setText(Integer.toString(length));
    modified.setText(date.toString());
  }
  catch(MalformedURLException e)       // just in case.....
  {
     System.out.println(e.getMessage( ));
  }
  catch(IOException e)
  {
     System.out.println(e.getMessage( ));
  }
  return;
}

public static void main(String[ ] args)
{
   Frame f = new Browser( );
   f.pack( );
   f.show( );
}
}
```

——————— 9.8 Summary ———————

This chapter demonstrates the ease with which Java can be used
to do a variety of networking jobs. It provides a very basic
introduction to the principles of data communication and client
server programming.

The **Java.net.Socket** class provides a quick and easy solution which will implement network connections regardless of platform. We don't have to worry if the remote computer is using Unix, Windows or even Macintosh as a platform, the JVM for that particular platform will ensure compliance.

Our first example, an Echo client and server establishes very basic principles. It doesn't take a huge stretch of the imagination to work out how the two programmes featured here could be altered to provide the basics of a 'Chat' program or Bulletin Board.

The HTTP Browser, similarly could be converted into a text-only Web browser by stripping the HTML characters out of the text.

9.9 Exercises

1. Rewrite the Client and Server programs giving them GUIs displaying messages in TextAreas and accepting destination addresses from a TextField.

2. Rewrite the Threaded Server with a GUI. (Hint: You will need to extend **Frame**, therefore you will implement **Runnable** instead of extending **Thread**.)

3. Write code that allows the client to close the connection by sending an an agreed word or character such as (Quit or Bye). The server should send the client the instructions for closing the socket at connection time, so that the user will know how to close it down gracefully. The code to close the socket is:

   mySocket.close( );)

4. Find out what other information can be discovered about a URL and implement a means of retrieving and displaying it. (HINT: **HttpURLConnection** is derived from **URLConnection**.)

10

DRAG RACING
– THE RACE

10.1 Aims of this chapter

The aim of this chapter is to deliver a working model of the drag racing game. The code for the GUI, we have already developed and is the same code we have seen elsewhere in the book. We still need to provide automotive powers to the cars and synchronise the race with the betting.

The code as presented here is not a finished version of the game. At the end of the Chapter I will suggest some structural improvements that you should be able to implement. When you have done that you will have developed a full scale working applet which can be embedded in Web pages and released to the Internet.

10.2 The Web page

We must supply some instructions to the players, and a good place to do this is the Web page in which the finished applet will be embedded.

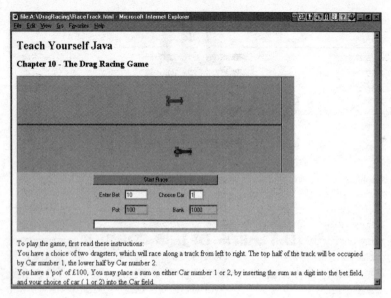

Drag racing in the browser

The applet is embedded in the Web page with this HTML code.

```
<HTML>
<BODY BGCOLOR="WHITE">
<H2>Teach Yourself Java</H2>
<H3>Chapter 10 - The Drag Racing Game</H3>
<APPLET CODE="RaceTrack.class" WIDTH=600 HEIGHT=325>
</APPLET>
<P>
To play the game, first read these instructions:<BR>
You have a choice of two dragsters, which will race along a track
from left to right. The top half of the track will be occupied by Car
number 1, the lower half by Car number 2.<BR>
You have a 'pot' of £100, You may place a sum on either Car
number 1 or 2, by inserting the sum as a digit into the bet field,
and your choice of car ( 1 or 2) into the Car field.<BR>
Press the "Start Race" Button to begin the action.
<P><i>last updated by Chris Wright on 17.8.97</i>
</BODY>
</HTML>
```

—————— 10.3 The program logic ——————

The program consists of two classes, one of which contains the other – the applet **RaceTrack** is a container for the **RaceTrackCanvas** class.

RaceTrack sets up the screen elements and triggers the initialisation of the **RaceTrackCanvas**. In addition to this, it runs the betting part of the game in a similar manner to our dummy run earlier in the book.

RaceTrackCanvas implements the **Runnable** interface in order to drive the animation. This causes the screen to be redrawn by successive calls to **paint( )** generated by the thread. The thread is started by the user clicking the "Start Race" button. An incrementing counter in the thread is used to supply the x position of the cars along the track, in combination with a random number between 0 and 5 which causes them to move at different speeds and allows one to catch up and overtake the other.

The **RaceTrackCanvas** class has its own initialisation method – **init(Applet app)**, which allows us to pass the applet an instance of our containing class so that we can communicate between the two. The position of each car is sent back to the **isWinner(int x, int y)** method of the **RaceTrack** class every time **paint( )** is called. When both cars have passed the finishing line, the thread is stopped and the winnings and losses are administered.

——————— 10.4 The code ———————

This is the complete code.

```
import java.applet.Applet;
import java.awt.*;

public class RaceTrack extends Applet
{
    // declare a variable of type RaceTrackCanvas
    RaceTrackCanvas animation;
```

```
// declare GUI elements
private Label betLabel, potLabel, bankLabel, carLabel;
private TextField betField, carField, potField, bankField,
  winnerField;
private Button goButton;
Panel p;

// Instantiate RaceTrackCanvas and set up GUI
public void init( )
{
   animation = new RaceTrackCanvas( );
   animation.init(this);
   setLayout(new BorderLayout());
   p = new Panel( );
   p.setBackground(Color.lightGray);
   GridBagLayout grid = new GridBagLayout();
   p.setLayout(grid);
   betLabel = new Label("Enter Bet");
   carLabel = new Label("Choose Car");
   potLabel = new Label("Pot");
   bankLabel = new Label("Bank");

   betField = new TextField(5);
   carField = new TextField(2);
   potField = new TextField(5);
   bankField = new TextField(7);
   winnerField = new TextField(20);
   potField.setEditable(false);
   bankField.setEditable(false);

   goButton = new Button("Start Race");

   GridBagConstraints gbc = new GridBagConstraints( );

   gbc.fill = GridBagConstraints.BOTH;
   gbc.insets = new Insets(5, 5, 5, 5);
   add(goButton, grid, gbc, 0, 0, 4, 1);
   gbc.fill = GridBagConstraints.NONE;
   gbc.anchor = GridBagConstraints.EAST;
   add(betLabel, grid, gbc, 0, 1, 1, 1);
   gbc.anchor = GridBagConstraints.WEST;
   add(betField, grid, gbc, 1, 1, 1, 1);
   gbc.anchor = GridBagConstraints.EAST;
```

```
      add(carLabel, grid, gbc, 2, 1, 1, 1);
      gbc.anchor = GridBagConstraints.WEST;
      add(carField, grid, gbc, 3, 1, 1, 1);
      gbc.anchor = GridBagConstraints.EAST;
      add(potLabel, grid, gbc, 0, 2, 1, 1);
      gbc.anchor = GridBagConstraints.WEST;
      add(potField, grid, gbc, 1, 2, 1, 1);
      gbc.anchor = GridBagConstraints.EAST;
      add(bankLabel, grid, gbc,2, 2, 1, 1);
      gbc.anchor = GridBagConstraints.WEST;
      add(bankField, grid, gbc, 3, 2, 1, 1);
      gbc.fill = GridBagConstraints.BOTH;
      add(winnerField, grid, gbc, 0, 3, 4, 1);

      betField.setText("");
      potField.setText("100");
      bankField.setText("1000");

      add("Center", animation);
      add("South", p);
   }
   // Helper method for GridBagLayout
   private void add(Component c, GridBagLayout grid,
        GridBagConstraints gbc, int x, int y, int w, int h)
   {
      gbc.gridx = x;
      gbc.gridy = y;
      gbc.gridwidth = w;
      gbc.gridheight = h;
      grid.setConstraints(c, gbc);
      p.add(c);
   }

   // Button starts Thread
   public boolean action(Event e, Object o)
   {
       if("Start Race".equals(o))
       {
          animation.start( );
       }
       return true;
   }
```

```java
// Check to see which car wins – called from RaceTrackCanvas
public void Winner(int x, int y)
{
   if ((x > y) && (y > 550))
   {
      play(1);
      animation.stop( );
   }
   else if ((y>x) && (x > 560))
   {
      play(2);
      animation.stop( );
   }
   else if ((x==y) && (x >560))
   {
      winnerField.setText("Dead Heat!");
      animation.stop( );
   }
}

// Administer winnings and losses
public void play(int x)
{
   int bet, pot, bank, car, result;

   winnerField.setText("");
   bet = Integer.parseInt(betField.getText( ));
   pot = Integer.parseInt(potField.getText( ));
   bank = Integer.parseInt(bankField.getText( ));
   car = Integer.parseInt(carField.getText( ));

   result = x;
   winnerField.setText("Winner is " + Integer.toString(result));

   if (result == car)

   {
      pot = pot + bet;
      potField.setText( Integer.toString( pot));
      bank = bank - bet;
      bankField.setText( Integer.toString( bank));
   }
   else
```

```
      {
         pot = pot - bet;
         potField.setText( Integer.toString( pot));
         bank = bank + bet;
         bankField.setText( Integer.toString( bank));
      }
   }
}

// A Canvas is required to display the graphics
class RaceTrackCanvas extends Canvas implements Runnable
{
   RaceTrack app;
   public Thread driver = null;
   Image Track, Car1, Car2;
   int XPos1,XPos2, YPos, progress, speed1, speed2;
   Image offscreen;
   Graphics buffer;

   // pass applet to the canvas so we can communicate
   public void init(RaceTrack parent)
   {
      resize(600,270);
      setBackground( Color.darkGray);
      /* we can now use Applet methods prefaced by app, as
      RaceTrack extends Applet. */
      app = parent;
      Track = app.getImage(app.getCodeBase( ), "Track.gif");
      Car1 = app.getImage(app.getCodeBase( ), "Redcar.gif");
      Car2 = app.getImage(app.getCodeBase( ), "Bluecar.gif");
      offscreen = app.createImage(600, 270);
      buffer = offscreen.getGraphics();
      buffer.setColor(Color.darkGray);
      buffer.fillRect(1,1,600,270);

      // initial position of cars
      XPos1 = 30;
      XPos2 = 30;
      YPos = 55;

      // start race at beginning
      progress = -1;
   }
```

```java
// Reposition cars and (re)start thread
public void start( )
{
   if (driver == null)
   {
      XPos1 = 30;
      XPos2 = 30;
      driver = new Thread(this);
      driver.start( );
   }
}

public void stop( )
{
   driver = null;
}

public void run( )
{
   while( driver != null)
   {
      // compute random number to move cars
      speed1 = (int)Math.floor(Math.random( )*5);
      speed2 = (int)Math.floor(Math.random( )*5);

      // increment counter and call paint( )
      progress++;
      try
      {
         repaint( );
         Thread.sleep(750);
      }
      catch(InterruptedException e)
      {
         System.out.println(e.getMessage( ));
      }
   }
}

// We want to pass speed variables into drawing method
public void paint(Graphics g)
{
```

```
      // paint next picture to the buffer
      paintRace(buffer, speed1, speed2);
   }

   public void update(Graphics g)
   {
      paint(g);
      // move buffer contents to screen
      g.drawImage(offscreen, 0, 0, app);
   }

   public void paintRace(Graphics g, int x, int y)
   {
   int w, h;

      buffer.setColor(Color.darkGray);
      buffer.fillRect(1,1,600,270);

      w = Track.getWidth(this);
      h = Track.getHeight(this);
      if ((w>0) && (h>0))
      {
         buffer.drawImage(Track, 0, 0, app);
      }

      w = Car1.getWidth(this);
      h = Car2.getHeight(this);
      if ((w>0) && (h>0))
      {
         // position is current position + counter +  random number
         Xpos1 = XPos1 + progress + x;
         XPos2 = XPos2 + progress + y;
         buffer.drawImage(Car1, XPos1, YPos, app);
         buffer.drawImage(Car2, XPos2, YPos +105, app);
         // call Winner via call to containing Panel(App)
         app.Winner(XPos1, XPos2);
      }
   } // end of method

} // end of class
```

10.5 Summary

The featured code is passable as a prototype, but there are many improvements that could be made to make the program more realistic, as well as more robust.

For realism, if we were to make a separate class for the car, with its own drawing methods we could easily make the application more lifelike by introducing skids (swapping for a rotated image and give the car a range of user selectable attributes geared to the performance. We could elegantly introduce different patterns of acceleration by triggering an additional random number to be added after a certain *Xpos* has passed. We could also introduce a sound file to play for the duration of the game. Try adjusting the scope of the random number, this may give more dramatic overtaking manoeuvres, but if increased too far will detract from the program's smoothness.

It would be relatively simple to make the track rectangular and have the cars do laps. The trick here is to substitute a rotated version of the car image and to shift the increment from *Xpos* to *Ypos* when a certain position is reached.

To speed the race up, implement it using clipping so that we don't redraw the background each time, and make the delay on the thread smaller.

For robustness, the essential thing is to make sure that the user inputs some numerical data, or to provide code that will do it but not count it as a valid bet. The reason for this is that we are passing the values in the fields, via a conversion routine, back into the program. If there is no value in the field, then we will get runtime errors.

At this point, we have moved suddenly into the realm of real world applications – you are now ready to take on the whole language. Remember that the Java API, often bundled with the distribution will yield answers to most of your queries, so long as you understand what you are trying to do. If the logic is wrong, nothing will save the program except patience, calm and a willingness to go back and start again.

APPENDICES

1 Java keywords

Keywords are reserved for specific purposes in a programming language and are not allowed for use as variable names.

abstract	boolean	break	byte
byvalue	case	catch	char
class	const	continue	default
do	double	else	extends
false	final	finally	float
for	goto	if	implements
import	instanceof	int	interface
long	native	new	null
package	private	protected	public
return	short	static	super
switch	synchronized	this	threadsafe
throw	transient	true	try
void	volatile	while	

2 Internet resources

Web sites

The web is an everchanging medium, and there are literally hundreds of Web sites with Java applets featured. I have restricted this list to a level higher – these sites can be looked on as gateways. If you know of any excellent site omitted from this list, please e-mail me at:

   tyj@chroma.demon.co.uk

http://www.unl.ac.uk/~cwright/tyj/
Contains a link to the site supporting this book and many more Java related sites.

http://www.javaworld.com/javasoft.index.html
A superb resource, magazine format contains code, advice, discussion.

http://java.sun.com/docs/books/tutorial/
Java tutorial with Sun's blessing

http://www.neca.com/~vmis/java.html
Shlurrrp....Java Tutorial

http://www.progsource.com/java.html
The Programmers' source....

http://www.digitalfocus.com/digitalfocus/faq/
The Java Developer

 http://www.developer.com/
The front door to the legendary Gamelan site

http://javaboutique.internet.com/
The Java boutique.

http://www.apl.jhu.edu/~hall/java/Welcome.html
Java Programming Resources

http://www.cs.cmu.edu/~jch/java/optimization.html#quotes
Java Optimisation

http://www.nebulex.com/URN/
Java Resource Network

http://sepc.twi.tudelft.nl/~sylvia/java/pointers.html
Resources for Java

http://www.seajug.org/html/resources.html
Java Related Resources

http://n106.is.tokushima-u.ac.jp/member/kita/info/java.html
Java Resources (Japan)

http://www.acme.com/java/
ACME Java - Excellent and informative resource

http://www.infospheres.caltech.edu/resources/java.html
Java Resources at Caltech

http://www.cupojoe.com/resources.htm
Cup O'Joe Java Resources

http://java.sun.com/products/jdk/1.1/docs/api/packages.html
The API reference for 1.1.3 (at the time of writing). Also
distributed with the download, so check that this is not already
on your hard drive.

Newsgroups

Of the many Java newsgroups, these two stand out for being
tolerant towards newcomers and having a large enough flow of
traffic to remain interesting.

Advice to beginners:

Just hang out and read the messages for a few days at first, the
chances are that something similar will have already been asked.
One good way to earn the hatred of everyone on a list is to ask
one of the FAQ questions. To avoid this, seek out and read the
FAQ for each list you subscribe to.

comp.lang.java.gui
comp.lang.java.programmer

INDEX